Mystery Mine

This Armada book belongs to:

Other titles by Màlcolm Saville in Armada:

Lone Pine series

Mystery at Witchend
Seven White Gates
The Gay Dolphin Adventure
The Neglected Mountain
Wings Over Witchend
The Secret of Grey Walls
Lone Pine London
The Secret of the Gorge
Not Scarlet But Gold
Treasure at Amorys
Man With Three Fingers
Strangers at Witchend
Rye Royal
Where's My Girl?
Home to Witchend

The Brown Family series

The Secret of Galleybird Pit
Good Dog Dandy

Buckingham series

The Master of Maryknoll
The Long Passage

Mystery Mine

Malcolm Saville

Armada

First published in 1959 by
George Newnes Ltd.
First published in Armada in 1979 by
Fontana Paperbacks, 14 St. James's Place,
London SW1A 1PS.

Printed in Great Britain by
Love & Malcomson Ltd., Brighton Road,
Redhill, Surrey.

Contents

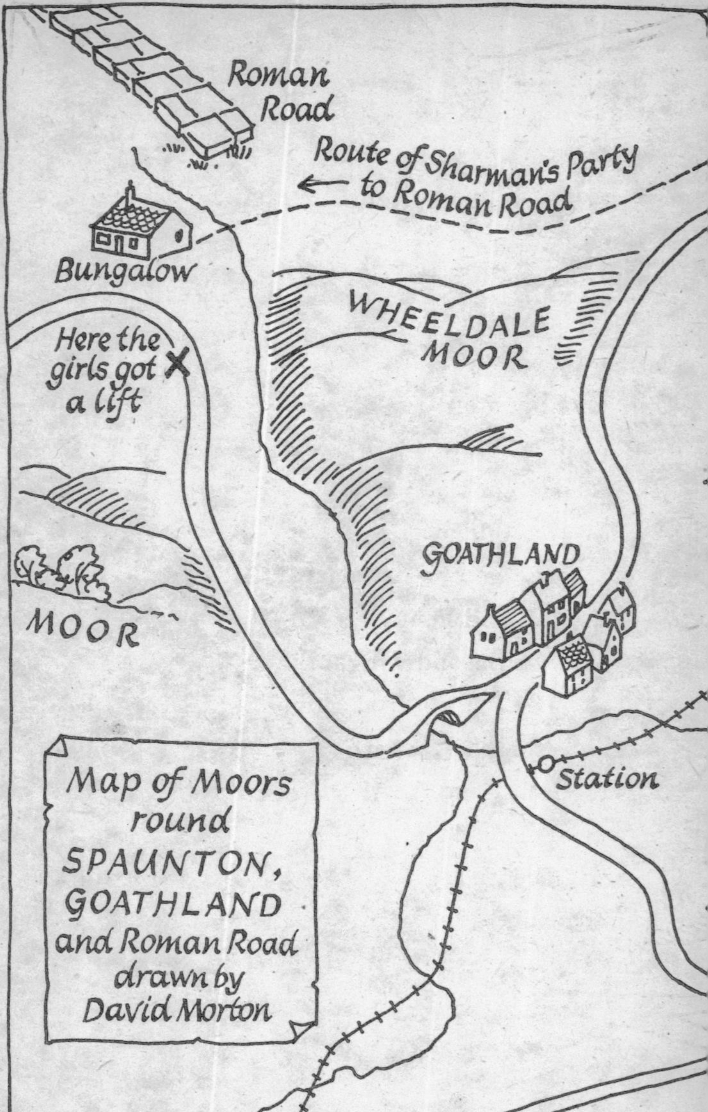
Roman Road
Route of Sharman's Party to Roman Road
Bungalow
WHEELDALE MOOR
Here the girls got a lift
GOATHLAND
MOOR
Station
Map of Moors round SPAUNTON, GOATHLAND and Roman Road drawn by David Morton

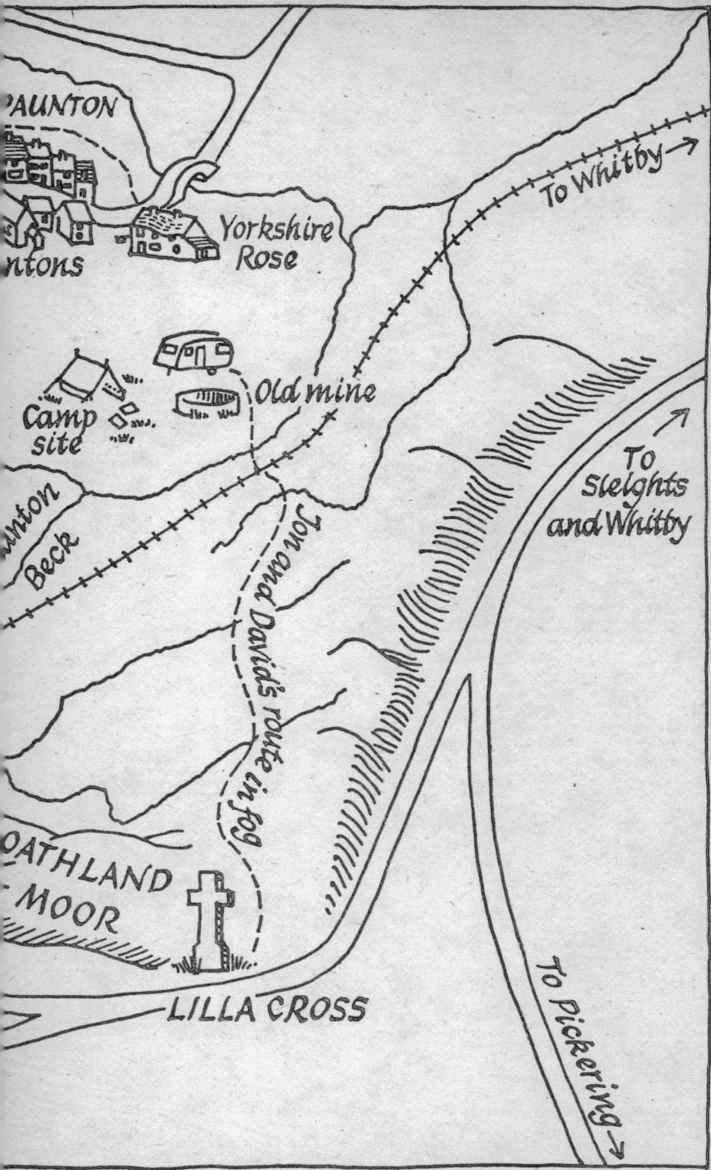

PAUNTON
Yorkshire Rose
ntons
To Whitby
Camp site
Old mine
nton Beck
Jon and David's route in fog
To Sleights and Whitby
OATHLAND MOOR
LILLA CROSS
To Pickering

Foreword

THE LONE PINERS featured in this story have already had many adventures in the Shropshire hill country, round Rye and Romney Marsh, on Dartmoor and in London. This time they find themselves in the wonderful moorland country in the North Riding of Yorkshire not far from Whitby and the coast.

Nearly all my stories are set in places to which you can go yourself, and if you ever go to Whitby or Scarborough or Robin Hood's Bay you will not be very far from these moors but, because this is only a story, I must explain which places are real and which are imaginary.

Whitby is real enough and, like the young man in the first chapter and Penny later on, you can sit on the quay and watch the fishing cobles come into harbour with the tide and then unload their slippery cargoes beside you. You can look across the water and see the curious old church on the opposite hill which can be reached by climbing one hundred and ninety-nine stone steps. Beyond the church are the ruins of the great abbey dedicated to St. Hilda. These places are real but you will not find Prospect Way nor the sinister little shop there.

Nine miles from Whitby, high on the moors, you will find Goathland as I have described it, but, so far as I know, there is no inn called *The Yorkshire Rose.* Pickering, away to the south, is real too and there was a railway line running from there to Whitby through Goathland.

I have walked along the Roman road where the Lone Piners were taken by Philip Sharman and you can do the same, realizing that you are treading where the Roman legions marched north from York. I am afraid that you will never find the "forgotten village" of Coram Street, although those of you who are interested in history and archaeology will find such a place miles away to the south of the county in the Wolds. It is called Wharram Percy and I have seen there the buried foundations of many of the houses of six centuries ago. There really is a "corpse way" running over the hill and you will also see a ruined church.

All the people in this story are imaginary, but the two villains appeared in the Lone Pine story called *The Neglected Mountain.*

I must also explain that this special edition is a little shorter than the original story which was first published in 1959, but the adventure, which I hope you will find exciting, has not been altered.

M.S.

THE PEOPLE IN THE STORY

John Robens	(Known sometimes as Charles Warner). A young scientist.
"The Doctor"	Nobody knows his real name nor what sort of a doctor he may be. Sometimes he calls himself Charles Williams.
Albert Sparrow	Elderly owner of an antique shop near Brownlow Square in North London.
George Venton	Another elderly owner of an antique shop in the village of Spaunton in the North Riding of Yorkshire.
The Two Miss Wildbloods	
Philip Sharman	A geologist.

And some of the Lone Piners and their relations and friends.

THE LONE PINE CLUB

The boys and girls known as the Lone Piners have had eleven previous adventures. If this is the first story you have read about them, you will probably enjoy it more if you know something about the Lone Pine Club which was founded at a lonely house called Witchend in the heart of the Shropshire hills.

The original rules of the Club are still hidden under the solitary pine tree in their first secret camp. They are very simple and are set out in full in *Mystery at Witchend*, which is the first Lone Pine story. All the members signed the oath in his or her own blood—*Every member of the Lone Pine Club swears to keep the rules and to be true to each other whatever happens, always.*

Here are the Lone Piners you will meet in this story:

David Morton is sixteen. He was elected captain of the Club when it was first founded. Lives in London. Not particularly brainy but above the average at work and games. Thoroughly dependable and a good leader.

Richard ("Dickie") Morton and Mary Morton are ten-year-old twins. Although the youngest members of the Club and often extremely irritating to the others, they have proved their worth in all the Lone Piners' adventures. Alike in looks and speech, they have a maddening trick of pretending to be younger than they are, and when in action together they annoy most grown-ups. They get their own way too often, but with all their faults they are warm-hearted, loyal and courageous and will tackle anything to justify themselves to the other members of the Club.

Jonathan Warrender is a few months older than David. He is tall and bespectacled and finds exams easy. Like many clever people he has little to say. He has no father, is still at boarding-school, and lives in the holidays with his mother who owns the *Gay Dolphin* Hotel in Rye on the edge of Romney Marsh. Here he first met the Mortons and had an adventure with them.

PENELOPE ("PENNY") WARRENDER is Jon's cousin and nearly one year younger. Her parents are abroad and she lives at the *Gay Dolphin* in the holidays. She is grey-eyed and red-headed, with all the qualities and defects that go with red hair—affectionate and impetuous, loyal and independent and a rare fighter for her friends and for what she believes to be right. Penny could never be described as a scholar but she is quick-witted and intelligent and a grand companion. In many ways she is old for her years, and for as long as she can remember the most important person in her short life, after her parents she so rarely sees, has been her cousin Jonathan. She teases and often infuriates him, but although she has not yet admitted it to herself, she would follow him to the end of the world.

PETRONELLA ("PETER") STERLING is just sixteen and the Vice-Captain of the Club. She was born in the Shropshire hills, still lives there and goes to school in Shrewsbury. She has no mother, brothers or sisters but there was never a girl less like an only child, for she is quiet, unselfish, brave and loyal. She hates towns and loves the country and all living creatures. She is tall for her age and slim with blue eyes, a clear brown skin and long fair hair. Peter met the Mortons on their very first adventure in Shropshire and they—especially David—are her closest friends.

1. *Prospect Way*

THE OLD TOWN of Whitby on the Yorkshire coast is built on two steep hills divided by the river Esk as it runs out through the harbour to the sea. The east cliff is crowned by the ruins of an abbey and there is also a church with a graveyard almost toppling over the edge. On the other side of the river is the quay where the fishing boats unload. High on the west cliff are plenty of smart hotels, flower beds and promenades, but between these modern streets and buildings and the quay, above which the seagulls swoop, is a tangle of alleys, courtyards and cobbled ways in which a man who did not want to attract notice could hide for many a long day.

One of these narrow streets is called Prospect Way. It is oddly named because it is not a way to anywhere, being but forty yards long. There is only one way in and no other way out. Prospect Way is a squalid and depressing backwater, and not even the early sun on a spring morning when this story opens was able to brighten it.

Half-way down on the left-hand side is a small shop which offers for sale newspapers, tobacco, ball-point pens and some tired-looking sweets, but it does not look as if anybody has bought anything there for years. There is a door into the shop on the left of the window and another on the right which is a separate entrance to the house.

In a small, drab room directly over the shop a young man was eating his breakfast. On the other end of the table were some books and a clip of newspaper cuttings and in the hearth stood a pair of heavy boots coated with dried mud.

The door opened and a woman wearing a dirty overall and soft slippers came in.

"Good morning, Mr Warner. I hope you found that bit o' fish tasty?"

"Thank you," the young man said coldly. "I used to like fish but this was cooked by your usual methods, I do not doubt. I have often thought that your cooking is unique. Has the post come?"

The woman wiped a hand on her overall and then produced an envelope from her pocket.

"Just this very minute, Mr Warner. Having done your breakfast I was just sorting through some of the papers in the shop when in comes the postman. Only this one for you today, though. Funny, isn't it? Got a Whitby postmark."

Warner took the letter from her hand.

"Thank you. I have all I need now that I have my letter. I'll call if I want you."

The woman went out after a curious look at her lodger who stared at the envelope for half a minute without opening it. He knew from whom the letter came because he recognized the handwriting, and knew too that he was not going to like its contents. He had been expecting it ever since he had received instructions to live in these squalid rooms.

Charles Warner was a strange-looking man. His clothes were shabby and there was a wild gleam in the dark eyes behind the heavy horn-rimmed spectacles. His hair was long and untidy and he wore a beard. The fingers of his right hand were stained brown with tobacco smoke. But his voice, and the pile of books and scientific papers at the end of the table suggested that he was an educated man.

He poured himself another cup of tea, lit a cigarette and then opened the envelope. There were only a few lines of handwriting on the unaddressed sheet of paper.

On the morning on which you read this the fishing fleet will come in with the tide at about 10 *a.m. Watch it from the seat nearest the shrimp stall on the quay and await further instructions.*

Warner sighed and burned the letter. He looked at his watch. Nine o'clock. It was not possible to judge the weather from the windows of the houses in Prospect Way but he could see that it was not raining, so without hat or coat he went down the dark, narrow staircase to the door leading directly into the street. He was not the sort of man who ever took much notice of what happened out of doors, but this morning he realized that the sun was bright, the sky clear and blue and the air keen. He strode out of Prospect Way and walked fast up the hill to the lawns and promenades of the West Cliff. It was not too early in the year for holiday-makers for Easter was but a week old, and for a while Warner sat on a seat on the cliff top.

Then he saw the fishing fleet coming in between the two arms of the harbour with each boat trailing behind it a thin, white ribbon of wake on the ruffled water.

At two minutes to ten he looked at his watch, shrugged his shoulders and walked down the steep, winding road which led to the crowded quay. Four fishing cobles were already moored and the fishermen, in blue jerseys and great rubber boots, were loading their catches into big wicker baskets. The baskets were then hauled on deck from the holds and swung on to the quay by another man who staggered with his load to an open-sided shed where the fish were weighed, sold and packed.

Warner lit another cigarette, pushed through the watching crowd and looked round for a shrimp stall. It was about thirty yards away nearer the swing bridge across the harbour. A man and a girl were sitting on the nearest seat.

Warner strolled across and joined them and they looked at him without enthusiasm. Warner leaned back, put his hands in his pockets and closed his eyes against the strong sunshine. He was roused by a hated but familiar voice.

"Pardon me, but could you oblige me with a light?"—and as he sat up with a start: "Don't be so surprised, Robbie. You're late. I've been watching and waiting for you."

Warner passed over the matches and looked at the man at his side. Everything was going to plan, but this was certainly a new disguise. The man known as "The Doctor" to those who worked for him, was of commonplace appearance and no disguise would ever really suggest anything else. He, too, viewed life through strong, black-rimmed spectacles and was thick-set with greying hair brushed back from a wide forehead. His face was normally florid and clean-shaven but he now had a straggling moustache.

Warner had seen him in many disguises and today he obviously thought that he looked like a holiday-maker. Warner shuddered with distaste at the sight. He was wearing grey trousers, a checked shirt open at the neck, a brownish-red sports jacket and a soft felt cap on the back of his head. He was also wearing sandals and smoking strong tobacco in his pipe.

"Now listen, Robbie. You're getting your orders now so don't miss anything as I've got to be off in ten minutes. And remember that I don't like being kept waiting . . ."

The other interrupted:

"I wish you wouldn't call me Robbie. You know that my name now is Charles Warner and I don't want to be reminded of the other. I only got your note this morning and if I'm late, no doubt it's because that woman in Prospect Way has more than half poisoned me. I can't stand that place, Doctor. It's filthy. I could be just as well hidden somewhere else."

"You'll stay there for the present, Robbie, if you please. You're in no position to argue. I'm paying you, and if what we're on to now comes off as I'm sure it will, we'll both be able to cut loose. I shall go to South America and you'll have enough to forget your other worries and start off on your research or whatever it is you want to do. And I shall call you Robbie just to remind you that your name when I first met you was John Robens and that is the name the police know, too."

"The police wouldn't mind knowing where you are either, Doctor," Warner muttered. "Anyway, cut the cackle and let me know what you've got to say as quickly as possible so that I can get away from the smell of whatever it is that you're smoking in that pipe."

The "Doctor" looked at him thoughtfully.

"You are a little over anxious and irritable, my dear

Robbie. Just be patient and let us work well together for the next month or two, because I am sure that the rewards are likely to be very great for us both. I cannot see that anything we are likely to do in the near future is likely to be actually against the law. We are pioneers, Robbie, and only people like us—me with drive, organizing ability and real brain, and you with the technical knowledge—are worthy of the rewards coming to us."

Warner laughed scornfully.

"Stop worrying, Robbie, and if you just do what you're told and keep in touch each day we shall do very well. There are others covering the north but I think that you will be the one to bring us the first good news."

"I wish you wouldn't speak as if you were doing me a favour," Warner replied. "You're talking too as if I was a public meeting. I'm prepared to see this last job through with you because I think it's important, and because we've agreed that if this comes off then we're both through with all this business for good. Now tell me what you've arranged."

"Very well. You will, for the present, stay in Whitby in the rooms I found for you, but if you get on the trail of what we are after you might stay at the local inn as a walker or holiday-maker. You are responsible for the country from Whitby to Pickering bounded by the coast to the east, and on the west by an imaginary line from Leasholm down to Lastingham in the south. All old mine workings of which there are many may be productive. I am particularly interested in such possibilities at a village called Spaunton, not far from Goathland. There should be the remains of a shaft on the moor very close to the village street. Try that first but there are many other prospects."

"Of course there are," Warner snapped. "Don't lecture me, Doc. I've said I'll see this through with you, but I wish you'd stop all this cloak-and-dagger business and disguises. Are the police after you?"

"I've told you not to mention police. I'm relying on you, Robbie. You're the best man I've got and together we can make a lot of money if all goes well. There's no sense in me being recognized."

"Suppose I want to get hold of you quickly?"

"Never mind where I am. I'll let you know where to come if I want to see you but I want a written report each day. Post to Charles Williams, care of the Post Office, Goathland."

Warner got up, pushed through the strolling crowds and leaned against the railings above the water. Then he lit another cigarette and stared across to the east cliff as the "Doctor" crossed to his side. He did not look round when the latter said:

"You know where you are now, Robbie, don't you? I'm on my way, but I should have told you that all the necessary equipment is being sent to you. Should arrive tomorrow and then you can get busy. Spaunton first. Don't trouble to follow me."

Warner answered without looking at him.

"Don't worry. I don't care for your company, Doc. Never did. Sooner this is all over the better it will suit me, but I do wish you'd stop playing the fool."

He glanced up with a look of disgust but the "Doctor" had gone.

2. *London*

ON THE SAME morning that Warner and the "Doctor" were sitting on the quay at Whitby, David Morton, a pleasant-looking boy of sixteen, crossed London's Strand and walked into Charing Cross station. He glanced up at the clock and then smiled cheerfully at the couple standing beneath it.

"Hello, you two. Sorry if I'm late. How was Rye looking this morning?"

The girl, Penelope Warrender, was a slim, pretty redhead. Her companion, her cousin Jonathan, was a few months older than David, three inches taller and wore glasses.

Penny, pink with excitement, spoke first.

"We've only been here a minute, David. We were the last off the train because Jon says that my case is filled with lead. Rye was looking lovely. How are you and the twins?"

"Twins are awful, Penny. I'm fine." Then to Jon: "How's everything, Jon? I've got a lot to talk to you about."

"Thank you *very* much," Penny said. "Don't you two mind me. I thought it might be a mistake for me to come to London. I try to be a refining influence on you both, but if you're not going to take any notice of me I might as well go home . . ."

Jon laughed and then said to David:

"Let's take Penny up to Brownlow Square so that she can do some refining work on the twins. Stand by to take turn with Penny's suitcase. Shall we go by bus or tube?"

"Bus, if we can get the cases as far. There's a stop on the other side of Trafalgar Square."

Brownlow Square where the Mortons lived was a forgotten corner of North London and it was not really a square because two of the sides were longer than the other two. All the houses were tall and narrow and the door of Number 7 to which David led his friends was scarlet—like a fire-station as his young brother Dickie said.

Jon and Penny had known the Mortons for a long time and indeed the family were their greatest friends. Mrs Morton came into the hall to greet them.

"Lovely to see you both. Lunch in half an hour. You're in Mary's room, Penny. You know that you're both welcome to stay here as long as you like."

They were still talking in the hall when the front door opened again and the twins and their Scottie dog, Macbeth, burst into the house.

Dickie and Mary Morton were astonishingly alike. They were dressed this morning in blue anoraks, shorts and rubber boots and both they and the dog were plastered with mud. When they saw Jon and Penny standing at the bottom of the stairs, Dickie clapped his hand to his head and staggered back against the closed door. Mary took her cue and staggered back too.

"Look at that, twin," Dickie gasped. "Do you see what I see? It's like a bad dream. Who do they remind you of?"

"Jon and Penny," Mary squeaked. "They look like those two from Rye only much, much cleaner, if you know what I mean."

"Unfortunately we do know what you mean, Mary," their mother said coldly. "Will you both please try to behave yourselves and take off your boots before you step off the mat. And please tidy yourselves up, for lunch is nearly ready. Hurry now."

When they had all helped to wash up after lunch, Mrs Morton took Penny out shopping while the twins went out to see their friend Harriet Sparrow, who was staying for a week or two with her grandfather who kept an antique shop a few streets away.

It was nearly tea-time when Penny walked into the sitting-room to find David and Jon crouched over the table examining some large-scale maps. They glanced up and said "Hello", and then looked a little awkward as she slipped into a big chair by the fire.

"There's something wrong with you two today," she said. "Have you made what the twins would call a plot? Now that we've got the rest of the holidays to ourselves what are we going to do with them? When are we going up to Witchend? I haven't heard from Peter for ages, but I suppose she's written to you, David?"

"Not for some weeks," David admitted as he sat on the edge of the table. "We were going to write to her or ring her up after you two came. We can't very well go to Witchend without the parents and I don't think they can manage it now until the summer. No reason why some of us shouldn't go though if we can stay at Ingles or Hatchholt."

Penny stood up and faced them.

"*Some of us?* What are you talking about, David? What does he mean, Jon?"

Jon pushed her gently back into the chair and sat on the arm.

"Don't get mad with us, Penny, but we both found this afternoon that what we want to do just for once is to go off on a hike on our own for about a week. We want somewhere we've never been to before and we'd like some rough climbing, too."

Penny looked at him as if he had hit her and then, to her fury, felt the tears in her eyes. She turned away so that neither of the boys should notice, but before she could reply Mrs Morton came into the room and sensing that something was wrong looked inquiringly from one to the other.

"You'd better tell your mother about your new plans, David," Penny said brightly. "I expect Peter would like to hear them too, but you and Jon must decide where and when you're going as soon as possible and then if you have time, do please let us know."

David, for once, looked annoyed.

"I've told you that we've only just thought of this," he reasoned. "It's an idea, that's all." And he went on to tell his mother what they were discussing.

The more he said the more ashamed of herself Penny felt. Before she could explain to Mrs Morton that what made her so mad was the calm way in which they made their plans without consulting anybody else, the twins came in.

"Harriet is coming to tea presently," Mary said. "She's just helping Mr Sparrow, but she says she's got something terrific to tell us. She wants to see Jon and Penny too."

"She'll have to hurry, then," Penny laughed. "Jon and David are going off on a hike somewhere on their own, twins, so it isn't likely that we shall all go to Witchend now. We've only been here a few hours but they've decided, and we shall have to think of something to do. I'd ask you all to come to the *Dolphin*, but my aunt is very busy there now just after Easter and there isn't room in the hotel. What a pity!"

"Is that true?" Dickie said quickly. "Are those two bullies really going off somewhere without us? Why, that's absolutely *fabulous*, Mary. Jus' think, twin. No more bossing about and pushing around. It's like a wonderful dream."

"Lucky, lucky us," Mary agreed, and then was interrupted by a shout from the hall.

"It's me, Harriet. Please may I come in?"

Mrs Morton whispered quickly to Penny, "I'll go and get the tea. Don't worry about this. They've got to go off on their own sometimes, but they'll always come back." Then, "Hello, Harriet. Nice to see you again. Stay to tea and tell us your news. How's your grandfather?"

"He's very, very excited, thank you, Mrs Morton, and so am I. Aren't you going to stay and hear my news? And thank you for asking me to tea."

Harriet Sparrow was twelve—slim, with an eager, pale face, wide grey eyes and dark, untidy hair kept in place with a narrow, velvet band. She was a romantic and imaginative person, an only girl who lived in South London with her parents. Each holiday she came to stay with her grandfather who lived over his second-hand shop near Brownlow Square. There was a great affection between old Mr Albert Sparrow and his granddaughter who had first met the Mortons and the Warrenders last Christmas.*

As Mrs Morton went out Harriet greeted Jon and Penny, then said excitedly, "*Now* can I tell you my exciting news? It's awful, really, because it will mean that I'm going—— Oh, all right then. I'll tell you everything from the beginning."

"That's a good thing," David said, rather relieved that there was now a chance of getting Penny interested in Harriet instead of Jon and himself.

Harriet ran over to the door to make sure that it was fast shut and then said in a piercing whisper:

"Last holidays, after our adventure, you promised that I should be a member of your Lone Pine Club. You all promised but it didn't happen 'cos there weren't enough to make me swear the oath or something. The twins told me all about it but I'm still not in it and I think I ought to be. We might have another adventure any minute and then where would I be. You do all want me to be in, don't you?"

They all explained that they did, but that the other members in Shropshire, who were all looking forward to meeting her, must agree too.

"You're onnery," Dickie explained. "It's a fabulous thing to be onnery, but you're it really. You're in the Club. Now tell us this terrific thing that you wouldn't tell us at your place and what it's got to do with Mary an' me."

Harriet looked round happily. This was her moment and she was tremendously proud to have them all as her friends. She made her speech.

"I expect I shall have to tell Mrs Morton all about this sometime, but I want you to know about it first. A most exciting thing is going to happen to me and it's all to do with my grandfather. I don't expect you know, but he was born in Yorkshire and although he's lived in London for years and years and years and had his shop here, he's always talking about going back to Yorkshire. David and the twins know that I only came to see him the day before yesterday

* *Lone Pine London*

but last night he told me what had been happening . . ."

She paused for breath and Mary protested:

"Well, what *is* happening, Harry?"

"Well, this is it," Harriet went on. "Grandfather has heard of a little shop full of lovely second-hand things like ours in a village in Yorkshire. It's a village called Spaunton where lots of tourists go, and the man who is selling it to Grandfather wants our shop here in London. So it's all very wonderful, you see! Grandfather wants to end his days in Yorkshire and wants a shop and what he calls a little piece of Yorkshire land, and the other man wants a shop in London and so they've seen each other's shops and they're going to exchange."

"We shan't like this at all, Harry," David said. "The new man may be nice but all of us Mortons like a Sparrow just round the corner. When is he going?"

"And what about you, Harry?" Mary said quietly. "If there isn't a Sparrow round the corner, you'll have to come and stay with us here every holiday, and anyway you'll have to come to Witchend soon to be made a proper member."

"What else?" Dickie hissed. "What about us?"

"I'll tell you. Grandfather is going up to Spaunton quite soon for about a month and the other man, Mr Venton, is coming here. They're going to exchange shops just to see that it works. Grandfather says it's a wonderful little house and shop and he wants me to go with him and stay until it's time to go back to school. He says that he would like me to have company and he wants Dickie and Mary to come too. Would you like to come, twins? Grandfather is coming to ask your mother presently."

The twins looked at each other and winked, and then danced round her in triumph.

"Fabulous, fabulous," Dickie chanted.

Harriet laughed and pushed them aside.

"There's another thing I thought of too. When we've seen what the village is like—the twins and me, I mean—I wondered whether some of you others could come up there too and p'raps we could have an adventure. Could we ask the others in Shropshire, although it is rather a lot, isn't it?"

Jon went over to the table and turned the pages of a road atlas. David joined him and Penny looked miserable.

"Here it is," Jon said. "Only just big enough to mark but it's on or near the Esk and not far from Whitby. Here's another small place called Goathland. Looks like good country. It's the moors of course and the Cleveland Hills. We might as well go up there for a few days and have a look round. I've never been to the North Riding, have you?"

As David shook his head, Penny went into battle.

"Of course you two had better go and have a look at the country and as far as I'm concerned you can stay there! It's different for the twins and I'm glad for them and Harry, but what about Peter and me! Isn't Peter expecting us at Witchend? I suppose David won't telephone her until he's absolutely certain when you're going! You're both so selfish that I'm ashamed of myself for knowing you, and if it wasn't for being rude to Mrs Morton who has just asked us to stay here as long as we like I'd go back to Rye." And with a toss of the head she made a grand exit towards the door. The others watched her in stupefied silence, but as she touched the handle the door was pushed open from the other side and Mrs Morton and Mr Sparrow came in.

Mr Albert Sparrow was charming. He was old-fashioned in his courteous habits and appearance, but he was an excellent business man with a wide knowledge and experience of glass, china, furniture and antiques. He did not approve of his only son's marriage but he loved Harriet and there was a great bond between them.

As soon as he followed Mrs Morton into the room his eyes went to Harriet and then to Penny who had nearly been hit by the opening door. He was a small man—rather like a perky sparrow—for his eyes were bright behind his glasses and his thinning white hair was in a sort of cockscomb on the top of his head.

Penny blinked back her tears as Mrs Morton, quick once

again to sense the difficult atmosphere, smiled at her. Then the twins ran across the room and Mary said:

"Harriet has told us, Grandpa Sparrow. She's told us everything. All we want to know now is when we can start because we're sure our mother will welcome us going . . . Nice quiet house without us, see?"

"We must ask your father when he comes home," their mother said. "It *will* be a nice quiet house without you, but we shall have to decide tonight because Mr Sparrow has had some more news about the shop—his new shop, I mean."

They all crowded round the old gentleman and it was obvious that he was enjoying the excitement.

"Well, my dears," he began, "I have received a telephone message from Mr Venton in Spaunton. He wants me to go up tomorrow or the day after. He tells me that he has received a very tempting offer for his shop. There is no danger that he will break his contract with me, but he is puzzled by this offer and wants to discuss the situation. When we have had our talk he will come south at once for we are both exchanging our businesses for a month."

"But will all this make any difference to the twins coming, Grandpa?" Harriet said. "If Mr Morton says 'Yes', p'raps we can go tomorrow. Mr Venton won't mind, will he? And will there be room in the house for us all?"

"There will be room and Mr Venton won't mind. He has just told me that he has a housekeeper who lives in the village and who will help us each day. There is also a caravan on the moor above the house. I do not suppose that Harriet has told you that I am buying Venton's place because with the house goes a few acres of the moor which comes down almost to the village street. I hope you will all see it one day."

3. Spaunton

THREE DAYS LATER, just before eleven o'clock in the morning, Jon and David got out of the train at Whitby, having travelled overnight to York.

"Do you think we were fools not to get out at Goathland?" David said. "We'd only have been a few miles from Spaunton by the look of the map."

"Of course not. I want to see the sea before we try the moors, and Spaunton can't be more than twelve miles from here. Let's leave the luggage in the cloak-room and look round this place."

The tide was out and the seagulls were still quarrelling over the muddy banks of the Esk when they reached the quay and sat on the seat by the shrimp stall. They bought some shrimps and munched them as David spread out the map on his knee.

"We should have to take the road to Guisborough, but turn south off it on the main road to Pickering after about two miles," he said. "If we could get a bus as far as this place called Sleights which looks to be at the bottom of a terrific hill where the river and the railway run along the valley, we should be able to walk across the moors to Spaunton. Or we could stay on the bus as far as Goathland."

"Looks all right," Jon agreed. "But there don't seem to be many tracks marked across the moor. The railway line here on the map is the way we've just come. The country is certainly wild, David. Looks as if this is going to be a good trip. We'd better buy some food because the weather is fine and we may as well make the best of it. There's no reason why we must sleep at Spaunton, is there? We can call anywhere we like as we've got the tents. The others aren't expecting us at any special time, but I'll be glad to know how they've got on. It's odd that old Sparrow should be so keen to settle in this one particular village."

"He's seen it," David said as he threw up some shrimps' heads which were caught by two swooping gulls. "He went up there before Harriet came to stay with him after Easter. He says that he wants a bit of his native county."

"There's no reason why we shouldn't have a day or two on our own before we join up with the others, is there?" said Jon. "They'll get on better without us."

David looked at him in surprise.

"We don't have to stay in Spaunton, Jon. We can just look them up and go on somewhere else. I want to let the parents know that the twins are all right . . . Wonder what Penny's doing?"

"So do I," Jon replied grimly. "She was cheerful enough when we left, wasn't she?"

"Cheerful but cool, I thought. Mother and Dad will give her a good time, and anyway there may be a chance of us going to Shropshire soon. If the twins and Harriet are settled in Spaunton, maybe we could take Penny and have a spell up at Witchend with Peter, Tom and Jenny."

"Perhaps?" Jon was doubtful. "I've got an odd sort of feeling that it isn't going to work out like that. I know Penny better than you do. She doesn't like us at present and I'm sure she's up to something . . . Now let's have another look at the map."

David's one-inch Ordnance showed them that they were on the edge of exciting country. The two main roads to the south—one to Pickering and the other to Scarborough—crossed high moors. Fylingdales to the east of the former: Goathland, Egton High and Wheeldale moors to the west. Spaunton could be seen not far from Goathland and it was David who noticed that "Old mine workings" were marked on the moor just by that village.

"That's odd. What sort of mine, I wonder? You don't think of them mining for anything up here, do you? This country looks even wilder than the Stiperstones. Wouldn't be lead, would it, Jon?"

"No idea. I'd heard there were old coal-mines over in the Dales on the borders of Westmorland, but that's miles away . . . Look, David. Here. South of Spaunton there's an old Roman road marked. It's not part of the main road but just wandering off across the moor on its own. That should be worth seeing. Let's do some shopping now. I'll send a postcard to Penny."

David laughed. "Good idea, but don't write 'Having a lovely time'. Say 'Wish you were here'. I'll send one to Peter and say just that. I must send one to the parents, too."

They did their shopping and posted their cards to London, Shropshire and Rye and then climbed the narrow streets up to the West Cliff and looked across the harbour to the old parish church and the ruins of the abbey beyond.

"I went to the library yesterday and read up this place," Jon said. "There's a good story about the abbey. Sort of story that Jenny would like. When the abbey was suppressed—Henry VIII I suppose, but I'm not sure—it was dismantled. The beautiful bells were sold and ordered to be taken to London. The bells were got safely aboard the ship, and all the people of Whitby came out of their houses and lined the harbour with awful wailings and lamentation. The sails were unfurled and the anchor weighed as the tide ebbed. The little ship moved slowly out of the harbour and then refused to carry its sacred burden further. Although it was a summer evening and nearly dead calm, the ship sank slowly and quietly beneath the gentle waves. And out there within sight of where we're standing now, the bells remain at the bottom of the sea."

"What happened to the unlucky crew?"

"Nothing was said about them. Now let's collect our rucksacks and get a bus either to Sleights or to the Goathland cross-roads. Got your compass?"

David nodded and as they walked back down the hill the sun went in and a sudden chill wind crept up between the hills and made them shiver. They did not have to wait long for a bus and the conductor was friendly and interested to know where they were going.

They told him they intended to walk to Spaunton across the moors and asked him where they should be put down.

"Ever been on the moors before, son?" he asked David. "Well, go careful. Spaunton's not more than five miles away from the Lilla Cross where we'll put you down. Maybe though, you'd better go to Goathland and walk down the lanes from there."

"Why not across the moor?" Jon asked. "If it's not more than five miles we can't miss the way. We know the direction and we've got a compass."

"You'll be wiser to walk from Goathland. Weather isn't too good and you don't want to be out on the moor in a sea roke. There's no sense in it. These rokes come up sudden and it's often as much as we can do to finish our journey."

Jon looked out of the window as the bus roared slowly, in bottom gear, up the long hill called Blue Bank. It was bright enough but the sun was not visible and he wasn't quite sure where to look for it.

"Thanks for the warning," he said. "We'll be careful, but all the same we'd like you to put us down at that Cross. What is a roke? Sort of mist?"

The conductor laughed shortly.

"Sort of mist, eh? It's a fog that comes in from the sea in a few minutes and often after a bright morning. You chaps'll please yourselves o' course, but I doubt there's a track right across the moor towards Spaunton. I'd advise you to come back to the road if the roke comes over and come as quick as you can. Many of the tracks are made by sheep and don't lead anywhere special, so do have some sense. Maybe it'll clear but I've been on this route for fifteen years and I should know it by now. Here's the Cross coming up now. Are you getting off or coming on to Goathland?"

"Here, please," David said as he folded the map. "I can see the way but thanks again for your warning."

The conductor helped them out with their rucksacks and they stood and watched the bus getting smaller and smaller in the distance. Then they looked round.

Apart from the road now looking like a white ribbon, a

few grubby sheep grazing on the grass verge and a stone monument about a hundred yards away on their right, there was nothing to see but rolling moorland. The horizon in each direction was bounded by the smooth, heather-clad hills. There were no trees and only a few refreshing patches of green broke the monotony of the brown heather, which in a few months would be purple.

"Not much doing, is there?" said David. "D'you think we ought to have gone to Goathland? Can't see what that chap was fussing about, can you?"

Jon looked over to the east knowing that a few miles beyond the desolation of Fylingdales Moor lay the sea.

"No, I can't. Weather seems all right although it's much colder than when we got out of the train this morning. Come over to the Cross and then look at the map again. Might be a good idea to get cracking. People who live up here must know more about it than we do"—and he led the way along a narrow track to the mound on which the old Cross stood. Then they looked at the map. There was no doubt as to the direction of Spaunton. If they walked straight north from Lilla Cross they could hardly miss it, but there was no track marked and, as Jon pointed out, the contour lines showed that they were going to have plenty of walking up and down hills.

"It can't be more than five miles," David said as he folded up the map. "What are we worrying about? Come on, Jon. Let's take a bearing on the compass now and get going."

Jon nodded but did not remark that the sun was not shining and that somehow, to him, the distant moors against the skyline looked a little hazy.

After two hundred yards the track they were following ceased to exist and they found themselves struggling through knee-high heather.

"Five miles of this will be enough for me," Jon laughed. "It looked smooth from the road, didn't it?"

They floundered on for another quarter of an hour but there was still no sign of a track. David, with the compass, took the lead but they did not say much because it was hard work up and down hill. After half an hour's walking, when they hoped that they had covered about two miles, they realized that they had no idea where they were. There was no road nor any landmark in sight except three trees on a distant hill-top.

"Let's eat," David suggested as he flopped down in the heather. "I'm beginning to see what the conductor meant when he told us about the sea roke. It wouldn't be much fun being caught out here in a fog. Here comes the sun again anyway."

Even as he spoke the weather brightened and the colours of the moor changed. Jon pointed up to a hovering speck in the sky and said, "Kestrel, maybe? That's the first bird we've seen since we left the Cross. Are we still on our course? Look at the map again . . . I think we're here, David. The trees aren't marked of course, but I believe that over the next hill we shall find the railway and a stream called Spaunton Beck. And you'll be wrong if you think that will take us to the village. It doesn't go anywhere near it. We shall have to cross the stream and make for those trees. This is getting more like a commando course every minute."

And that was the last feeble joke either of them made for some hours. They scrambled down a steep hill into a valley and found Spaunton Beck deeper and wider than they expected. They scrambled across some big rocks and then crossed the railway track and took a line on the little clump of trees on the crest of the hill and started to clamber up towards it. The heather was thick and tall and as they struggled up neither noticed that the sun had vanished again. And more than the sun disappeared, for when they were nearly up, David looked round for the trees. To his astonishment they were no longer there. Neither was the skyline of the moor behind them. Suddenly it was cold, as the dreaded sea roke came sweeping in from the coast like a grey and silent ghost.

Jon looked round in astonishment.

"So that chap was right and we're the mugs. Taste it on

your lips, David. It's salt. We must find those trees."

As they climbed upwards the roke eddied round them, and when at last they sighted the trees and looked back, the beck in the valley had vanished. Indeed, all they could see twenty yards below them was a soft, but impenetrable blanket of fog. It was lighter on the top under the three stunted hawthorns—light enough for them to realize that all the colour had disappeared from heather and sky. And it was suddenly so cold that they shivered as the fog swirled round them.

The next hour and a half was very unpleasant and both boys admitted later that there were times when they were very scared. The fog never cleared, but occasionally, when they were high, the visibility improved. Jon carried the map while David tried to keep a course with the compass, but the only clues they had to their position were the valleys into which they were constantly descending and the becks they had to cross before they climbed up again. In ten minutes their shoes, socks, shirts and sweaters were sodden and they changed the latter for their waterproof wind-cheaters. Their hair was soaking and Jon constantly had to wipe his spectacles. At no time during this nightmare journey did they find even the semblance of a track. Time and time again they stumbled into holes hidden by the sodden heather and fell heavily, and as David said, when he had picked himself up for the fifth time, "I can't think of anything as unfunny as trying to get up out of this muck with a heavy rucksack on my back. Are we getting anywhere, Jon?"

"Well, we've been walking somewhere for an hour and a half," he said. "I don't believe we've been going round in circles and I'm sure we've done at least three miles so we can't be far from Spaunton. If we're where I think we are on the map, we're in the last of the valleys before we find the village. See what I mean?" And he pointed at the map.

"Yes, I do. The road through Spaunton runs down into a very steep valley and we may fall into that if we're lucky. There's also the little matter of the old mine shaft, David.

Here it is on the map. Almost right on top of the village by the look of it. That's another little hazard. Come on."

They toiled with dragging feet up the side of the valley and when they reached the top, the fog seemed thinner. Again David used the compass and five minutes later they saw two still and upright figures a few yards apart looming through the mist in front of them.

"Hello there!" David shouted, but his voice was muffled and there was no answer to his hail.

Jon strode ahead. "We're not getting full marks for intelligence today, David," he called back over his shoulder. "These are old wooden posts! There was a wire fence here once although it's rusty and broken up now. We must be near something."

David laughed as he joined him.

"Could be Spaunton. Go carefully in case we run into that mine shaft. Better follow the slope down. I believe I can smell wood smoke."

Five minutes later something else loomed up ahead of them, and they knew they were safe when they realized that they had found the shaft of an old mine surrounded by a circular wall of stones about twelve feet across.

Jon leaned cautiously over the wall and looked down into black emptiness. "It's like a well," he whispered. "I suppose they had a sort of winch or windlass over the top once and hauled up baskets of coal. How did they get it down to the road, I wonder?"

"Horses or donkeys, I suppose, but there ought to be a track leading downhill from here. Chuck a stone down, Jon. Perhaps the shaft is filled up now? If it isn't, it's certainly very dangerous."

Jon reached for a stone and then, as the mist cleared slightly, he saw something unusual on the opposite side of the wall.

"What's that, David. There's something hanging down the shaft . . . Hi! Look at this. It's a rope ladder. No it isn't. It's made of nylon or something like it."

They looked at each other in amazement. The top of the

light, workman-like ladder was held in position by steel hooks clamped over the firmest stones in the wall.

"Throw the pebble down now," David whispered. "Must be somebody down there."

Jon picked up a small stone and then dropped it at his feet. "Don't want to brain anybody," and then leaning over the parapet he shouted, "Hi! Anybody down there?"

His voice boomed and echoed down the shaft and although they listened carefully the only sound to break the silence was the distant drip of water far below.

"Very odd," Jon said. "Maybe it's some of those pot-holing chaps?"

David shouted down the shaft again but only the echoes came back to them. "None of our business, I suppose, but it seems peculiar to be exploring an old mine on a day like this. And there might have been an accident down there! Let's get down to the village and tell somebody. Now that we've got here, the fog is clearing."

They could see now that a rough grassy track, once wide enough for a horse and cart, led away from the mine shaft, so they followed this as it descended in gentle twists and turns round the contours of the hill. After they had been walking for five minutes, Jon pointed to a big, shapeless bulk shrouded in fog, about fifty yards from the track on their right.

"I think it's a caravan," he said. "It's probably the one belonging to Mr Sparrow so we shouldn't be far off now."

And so they came to Spaunton. A path ran down the steep hill from the caravan to a tidy vegetable garden, and suddenly the moor ended and they saw the grey stone houses of the village just below them.

The village of Spaunton was on two levels. Five shops, including Venton's, about thirty cottages and a petrol station were at the top of the steep hill, while the church, an attractive inn called *The Yorkshire Rose* and a few more cottages were half a mile away on the banks of a swiftly running river at the bottom. Behind these houses the moors fell so sharply to the water that the face of the cliff was too steep to be climbed.

The mist was still clearing as Jon and David hurried through the garden. The windows at the back of the house were curtained and they saw no sign of life.

"Let's get round to the front and see whether the shop is open," Jon suggested, so they followed a stone-paved path round the side of the house and past the back door into the village street.

Several people were about and an old man looked at them curiously as they turned to the right and looked, for the first time, at the famous little shop known as Venton's. The boys peered through the glass but the inside of the shop was dark and they could not see anybody there. Not much was shown in the window but in the centre was a superb gilt clock about eighteen inches high. On its right was a huge rose bowl patterned in vivid blue, red and gold and on its other side were some beautiful snuff-boxes. And that was all.

"Very, very expensive and exclusive," David said. "But how will he make a living here? Tourists, I suppose. This place must be very well known. Let's try the door."

They stepped into the shop on to a soft carpet. It was rather gloomy and they were just wondering what to do, when a door opened behind a curtain at the back of the shop, and Harriet switched on the lights.

"Good afternoon," she said politely, and then realized who they were. "It's Jon and David," she shouted over her shoulder, and the twins pushed past her followed by Macbeth who greeted David hysterically. Then Mr Sparrow appeared.

"My dear boys! I am delighted to see you. Come in and have some tea and tell us of your adventures."

"We'll be glad to get the rucksacks off, but we've got something urgent to tell you," Jon said.

"You're dropping mud and water on the carpet," Harriet laughed. "Come outside and I'll show you the back door."

She led them round the side of the house to the door they

had passed a few minutes ago, into a stone-flagged kitchen.

"Something has happened to you two," Mary said suddenly. "We know it has. You got lost in the fog, didn't you? Are you hurt or have you had an adventure?"

"Not really, Mary," David said as he slipped out of the heavy rucksack and stretched his arms and shoulders. Then he turned to Mr Sparrow.

"Do you know that old mine shaft up on the moor beyond your garden, sir?"

"I do. It's on my ground. It's dangerous and I have forbidden these children to go there."

"There's somebody down there now anyway," Jon said. "There's a nylon ladder hanging from the top and although we shouted there was no answer. We wondered whether we ought to tell the police or fetch help in case there's been an accident. Are people allowed to go down there? We wondered if it was pot-holers?"

"Nobody is allowed to go down that shaft. It's not safe. It's on private ground, too, and when I am able I'm going to repair that fence. Forgive me, but are you really sure about the ladder? It was foggy when you were up there."

"We're quite sure," David said shortly. "Why not come and see for yourself, Mr Sparrow? If you've got a good electric torch, that would be useful, and maybe some rope."

"I'm sorry, my boy. I'm sorry to have doubted you. Just allow me time to put on my boots and then we will go immediately. Harriet, there is a torch on the hook behind the door. If there is anybody down in the mine I shall certainly prosecute them for trespass."

The twins and Harriet ran for their rubber boots, and five minutes later, after Mr Sparrow had locked up the shop, they were all on their way up to the moor again.

As they passed the caravan, Mr Sparrow said, "You may sleep here, boys. It's all in order. All clean and comfortable. Stay as long as you like . . . Ah! The roke has cleared now and we can see the shaft. Richard, Mary and Harriet are to keep well back from the old wall . . . Now boys, let us examine this ladder."

But the trespasser—if there had ever been one—had gone and taken his ladder with him. Jon and David looked at each other in astonishment. They knew they had both seen the ladder hanging down into the dark depths of the shaft. It seemed hardly possible for anyone to have climbed up and taken the ladder away, and then to have disappeared, in so short a time, but then Jon looked at his watch and realized that they must have been away half an hour.

"Sorry to have brought you up here, sir," he said, "but there *was* a ladder. The hooks scratched the stones. You can see the marks. Look, David."

They all crowded round and Mr Sparrow forgot his instructions to the twins and Harriet. He peered at the wall and then declared that he could not see any scratches.

"But I can!" Dickie protested loyally. "You just look carefully, Grandpa Sparrow. I can see scratches."

Mr Sparrow looked steadily at Jon and David.

"There is nothing more we can do here. We do not know the depth of this shaft, but I intend to have it covered with wire or boarded over as soon as possible. I must ask you all, while staying here, to keep away from it."

While he was speaking, Macbeth was sniffing at the wall and the ground beneath it.

"Wish he was a bloodhound," Mary said. "He's very, very clever, but he isn't really a good trailer. I s'pose whoever it was isn't dead down there?"

"Don't be ridiculous, child," Mr Sparrow said sharply.

"Come along! Come along! Never mind about the old mine now. You boys are tired out and must have some tea. Harriet and the twins had better run back to the house and put the kettle on. The estimable Miss Wildblood said she would look in at six to see if she could help."

Jon and David were now so tired that they were glad to walk slowly back to the house with Mr Sparrow while the others ran ahead.

"Who is Miss Wildblood?" asked Jon.

"A most excellent person in spite of her name. She lives across the street, was Mr Venton's housekeeper and continues with me. We will ask her to provide a celebration supper this evening."

An hour later they were all at tea round the wood fire in the low-ceilinged living-room behind the shop when Miss Wildblood arrived. She put her head round the door, saw David and Jon and withdrew to the kitchen, but not before the boys had formed the opinion that Wildblood was a suitable name for her. She was tall and thin with wild, black hair and wild, black eyes and a swarthy complexion.

"How very fortunate," Mr Sparrow said. "Excuse me."

When he had gone out, Harriet said. "Isn't she peculiar? We think she's a witch, but she's a super cook and she's kind to Grandfather."

And it was a good meal that Miss Wildblood served later. Afterwards Jon and David could hardly keep awake, but they all jumped when the door-bell shrilled. Mr Sparrow got up and walked through into the shop, leaving the door ajar. The others, curious to know the identity of the visitor, stopped talking and listened. They heard the door open and a man's voice say, "Good evening, sir. If, as I believe, you are Mr Sparrow, may I ask you for a few minutes of your time? I would not bother you now if the matter I have to discuss was not extremely urgent."

They heard Mr Sparrow mumble a protest, and then came the sound of the shop door closing and the man spoke again.

"I will not keep you long, but what I have to say is definitely to your advantage."

Mr Sparrow came back to the living-room door and said, "Please excuse me. I will see this man in the shop. Do not interrupt me."

David got up. "Let's clear away and wash up before Jon and I fall asleep. And keep away from the door, twins. Mr Sparrow's visitor is no business of ours."

When they had finished in the kitchen, and realized that Mr Sparrow was still talking to the mysterious visitor, the twins slipped out of the back door. There were no street lamps in Spaunton, but the grocer's shop was next to Venton's and the windows were lighted.

"Let's hide in the doorway," Dickie whispered. "Why are you so keen to find out about this man, twin?"

"It's silly, but the voice reminded me of somebody we know, or somebody we once met. I just want to see him, Dickie. I think Grandpa Sparrow is worried about something although he's so happy up here in this fabulous place . . . Here they come. I can hear them at the shop door."

"I will see you tomorrow then, Mr Sparrow. The offer cannot remain open indefinitely and you will be very wise to accept it."

The door closed and the footsteps of Mr Sparrow's visitor came nearer. For a few seconds they saw him clearly—a tallish, shabbily dressed young man, bareheaded, with untidy black hair, a beard and a wild look in his eyes behind heavy, horn rimmed spectacles.

They stood back in the doorway but he stared at them as he passed. When his footsteps had died away down the hill, they stepped out into the road and Dickie said, "Did you see his boots, twin? Sort of climbing boots and they were all covered with grey mud. How peculiar."

4. *The Mine*

NEXT MORNING Jon and David slept late in Mr Sparrow's caravan on the edge of the moor. They were still asleep on the two bunks when there was a bang on the door and Harriet and the twins came in.

David sat up suddenly and rubbed his eyes.

"Get out," he mumbled. "Where am I? Get out and go away."

Harriet slipped behind the twins and closed the door.

"It's no use getting mad and red in the face, David," Dickie said. "You're all wrapped up in a sleeping bag and you can't get at us. We've come on very important, urgent, private, confidential business."

"O' course we didn't think that you would still be wrapped in sloth," Mary went on. "It's nearly nine o'clock and we've had our breakfast."

"Shut up!" Jon shouted.

"Please, please," Harriet pleaded. "Please don't be wild with us, Jon and David. We really have got something important to tell you. If you'll just sit there for a while we'll tell you all about it, and then, while you're dressing, we'll go back and get your breakfast. *Please* listen to us."

"All right," he said. "Five minutes only because we want our breakfast and if you twins are being funny . . ."

"I'll speak first," Harriet began. "It's about what happened last night and some peculiar things that have been happening to my grandfather since we came here. I get up early every morning and help with the breakfast, and if I wake up in time I take him a cup of tea. I did this morning and I could see that he was very worried and unhappy. I know when he's worried and the twins noticed it at breakfast because he hardly said a word. We've been talking about it secretly and we think it's something to do with that man who came to see him last night."

"But what can we do to help him, Harry?" David said. "I suppose that chap came about business and that's nothing to do with us."

"Ha!" said Dickie loudly. "Now you listen to us 'cos once again we've found out something. We just wondered about that man when we heard him speak to Grandpa Sparrow—you heard him too because the door was open—and so we went out into the street and did a bit of spying—"

"So that's where you went," Jon interrupted, giving Dickie a kick through his sleeping-bag. "Nosey as usual. What did you find out?"

Mary flushed.

"I s'pose it was rather nosey but Dickie an' me both thought we'd heard that voice before. You may think that's silly, but when he spoke it reminded us of somebody. We've tried to remember but we can't. You must know how things like voices or smells remind you of something."

"All right, Mary," David agreed. "We know what you mean. Did you remember him when you saw him outside?"

His sister gave him a grateful glance for taking her seriously, and went on to tell them how they had stood in the doorway of the grocer's shop, and heard the stranger say something about accepting a good offer.

"We did just see him, but it was only for a second, as he went down the street . . . It's most peculiar, David and Jon, but we *do* think we've seen him before. He's taller than Jon. He wasn't wearing a hat or a coat and his clothes were untidy. So was his hair—all wild and straggly. He glared at us as if he didn't like twins. He had thick, black specs on and a beard too."

David opened his mouth to reply but Dickie spoke first.

"And there's something else he had more important than a beard or specs let me jolly well tell you. He had big boots on—sort of climbing boots—an' they were covered with dried mud. Sort of white mud."

"Were they though?" Jon said. "It was very bright of you to spot that, Dickie."

"He might have been the stranger who had been down in the mine," Harriet broke in excitedly. "Don't you see that? And if he was, what has he got to say to Grandfather that worries him? Do you think we could ask Grandfather about it and say we think that man had been down in the mine?"

"Yes, I do," David said. "Get off my feet, Mary, and run and put the breakfast on like a good girl. I wish you could remember whether you really have seen this chap with the beard before—"

"Beards grow on and beards come off," Jon interrupted. "P'raps he hadn't got a beard when you saw him before and that's why you're puzzled about him. Anyway, you've never been to Yorkshire before so it isn't likely that you have seen him. Now what about our breakfast—"

The twins and Harriet scurried back to the house while Jon and David got dressed. It was a fresh, clean morning when they left the caravan. The moor was a warmer shade of brown than they had yet seen it, and the grass of the old track was fresh with the promise of spring as they walked down to the house. When they opened the kitchen door they were greeted by clouds of blue smoke and the delicious smell of frying bacon. Harriet and Mary were round the stove and Dickie was looking on admiringly.

David and Jon had nearly finished their meal when Mr Sparrow came in from the shop and greeted them. When he had asked them whether they were all going out for the day because it was fine, and they had thanked him again for the shelter of the caravan, the old man said suddenly, "Will the twins and Harriet please excuse us for a few minutes. There is something I wish to speak about to Jonathan and David—privately."

Harriet gave David a meaning look and led the protesting twins from the room.

Mr Sparrow sat down on the end of the table and they realized suddenly that Harriet was right. He was looking worried and old.

Jon spoke first. "You look tired, sir. Is there anything we can do to help?"

"Thank you, Jonathan. I know David better than you, but you are two sensible lads and as you know something of my affairs, I felt I would like to tell you of my visitor last night. I am concerned at the turn of events."

"We've been wondering whether the chap who called here last night is the same man who was trespassing in the mine when we arrived. The twins saw him outside and told us that he had mud on his boots," David said.

"So he did, my boy. So he did. He left marks on the carpet in the shop. It would be helpful to know for certain whether this man was exploring the old mine. I would like to know more about him."

"But why? What has he done?"

"His name is Charles Warner and he is staying at the inn called The Yorkshire Rose at the bottom of the hill. Last night—and remember we had never met before—after a few minutes' general conversation he offered me a very large sum of money for this business, the house and the land that goes with it. He said that he was acting for somebody else and could provide the highest references but that the offer was genuine. What perplexes me is the certainty that he knows nothing about antiques or the many treasures I have taken over from Mr Venton. He also wanted to look over the house and cellars."

"*Are* there cellars?" Jon asked quickly.

"There is *a* cellar, my boy. We store some stock down there and it is quite dry. No. I do not intend to sell Venton's. I have waited all my life for some Yorkshire soil of my own and here I am going to stay. I am anxious to know why somebody else should want this place so desperately. I was wondering whether I should go to London to discuss it with Mr Venton because he is, in some way, concerned. I would like to know more of Mr Warner—"

"Leave that to us," David said as he got up. "We would like to know more about him too."

Mr Sparrow then went back into the shop, and Jon and

David called the others and walked up to the edge of the moor just beyond the garden and sat down in the heather. David told them what had happened.

"Why don't you twins and Harriet go down to the inn and see if you can find out anything about Mr Charles Warner? I'm sure Mr Sparrow will never sell Venton's but some people seem to be pressing him hard to do so. There must be something special about the place. Are you still sure you've seen Mr Warner before, Mary?"

She nodded. "We both are."

"What are you two going to do?" Dickie said suspiciously.

"We're going to be about here," David smiled. "We'll talk to Mr Sparrow and keep an eye on the mine, and maybe we'll stroll down the hill and see how you're getting on. Don't get into trouble but you might be able to discover more than we can."

Dickie nodded. "All right. Come on, Harry. We don't think you've ever ever seen us do this sort of thing before. Come on, twin. And Mackie."

They hurried along the track to the village street and turned right down the steep hill.

"S'pose you ask at the Rose for him and he's there, what will you say to him?" Harriet asked.

"I don't know yet," Dickie replied. "It's not a thing we know until it happens, Harry. Maybe you'd better not say anything unless one of us asks you the question. It's not that you couldn't answer, o' course. It's just that you don't know how we make people livid and make them say things."

"I see," Harriet said. But she really did not.

Round a sharp corner they saw *The Yorkshire Rose* just beyond a narrow stone bridge at the bottom of the hill. A man was sitting on the parapet of the bridge.

"It's him. It's him!" Mary hissed. "Super luck, if he doesn't run away. Heel, Mackie!"

Dickie gave his sister a quick grin and whispered to Harriet, "When you speak to him, be very, very friendly . . . See his boots? He doesn't even trouble to get the mud off."

As the children strolled on to the bridge, Warner lighted a new cigarette from the stub of the last and then stared at them as if he loathed all boys and girls and this trio in particular. He was wearing old corduroy trousers and a heavy sweater, and at his feet was a rectangular leather case with straps which looked as if it might contain a big cinema camera. Macbeth ambled over and sniffed at the case and Warner shouted, "Get out! Keep your dog under control."

Mackie, with his head on one side, looked up at the man and then growled at the menace in his voice. Dickie called the dog, who came over obediently, and then the three children leaned against the parapet on the opposite side of the bridge and stared at Warner.

Mary spoke first.

"Good morning. There is no need for you to shout at our dog. He is friendly to people he likes, and growls at those who are rude to him . . . Are you staying here?"

Warner frowned.

"And what is that to do with you? Who are you?"

"We're twins," Dickie explained, rather obviously. "And this is our friend, Harriet." He nearly said Harriet Sparrow but something told him that it would be wiser not to give her surname yet. He was not yet sure whether Warner had recognized them from last night.

"I can see you're twins. Where have I seen you before?"

"We're not very famous," Mary said. "Acksherley we live in London but we like it very much in Yorkshire. We only asked you if you were staying here because it's a nice place and we like to be friendly. Why weren't you friendly to our dog? It's funny, but he seemed to like you."

Warner did not think this was funny.

"Well, I don't like dogs and I don't like you three standing there gaping at me. Please go away and don't bother me."

"*Bother you!*" Dickie said in hushed, shocked tones. "We're not bothering you and you're not bothering us either. We like speaking to you. What have you got in that leather case? Is it a squeeze-box?"

"A *what*?" Warner snarled.

"A squeeze-box. A concertina or a—what's the name for it, Harriet?"

"Accordion," Harriet said quietly. "I don't think this gentleman has got one of those in that smart leather case, twins. It's not the right shape. Is it a big camera? Are you one of those men who take photos of people at the seaside?"

Mary flashed her friend a look of admiration, but before she could speak Warner slipped off the wall and then stepped threateningly towards them. Then he stopped in the middle of the road and glared at the twins.

"I've seen you two before," he said quietly. "Sure of it. You live in London, do you? What are you doing in this place and why are you pestering me?"

"We're here on holiday and I suppose you are too. Have you got a paint-box in that case? Do show us, please."

"I will *not* show you and I forbid you to go near that case. Where have I seen you twins before?"

Dickie was frowning and trying desperately hard to imagine what the man's face would look like without his beard. The voice was still memorable and, in a hazy way, so were the glasses and the shock of black hair. They were not really getting anywhere and so the boy decided to take a chance by telling him who they were.

"We don't mind telling you about us. It's just that we wondered who you were. We only want to be friendly. We're staying at Venton's with Mr Sparrow."

Mary gave a beaming smile as she held out her hand. "You must be Mr Warner who came to see Mr Sparrow. Now we know each other. How do you do?"

Warner, with a dazed look in his eyes, shook hands with them all and then, realizing what he had done, he stepped back and scowled.

"You've forgotten to introduce me," Harriet said. "I'm Harriet Sparrow and my grandfather has just bought Venton's."

This information did interest Warner, who changed his tactics and asked them if they would like to sit on the seat outside the inn and have a soft drink. They thanked him politely and sat in the sunshine while their host went indoors with his heavy leather case.

"He wants something from us," Mary whispered. "Now he knows who we are he thinks we'll tell him things. You were marvellous, Harry, but think carefully before we answer any more of his questions. Have you remembered who he is, twin?"

"I'm in torture," Dickie muttered. "Absolute monstrous torture. My brain goes crack, crack, crack, but nothing else happens. Look out. Here he comes with the orangeades."

Warner asked them all sorts of questions about the house. He asked whether there were many cellars and he wanted to know how long Mr Sparrow had owned the business and what had happened to Mr Venton. Then he had the impertinence to ask Harriet whether her grandfather had enough money to live comfortably, and although she was very angry she managed not to answer any of these questions. Warner then suggested that a winter in a village like Spaunton would be much too severe for an old man like Mr Sparrow, and to that Harriet replied angrily, "My grandfather is a Yorkshireman and he knows all about winters. What do you know about Yorkshire winters? You don't speak like a Yorkshireman. My grandfather knows exactly what he's going to do, thank you."

Warner looked surprised but did not seem to take offence and then asked her where she lived and went to school.

"I'm staying with my grandfather at present," she said stiffly. "And anyway I can't see what it's got to do with you. I don't want any more of my drink, thank you," and she got up and glared at the twins fiercely.

"There's no need to upset yourself," Warner sneered. "A few minutes ago you said you all wanted to be friendly, and when I ask you some friendly questions you get in a rage. Silly kids! Go away and leave me in peace and tell your grandfather that I shall be coming to see him early this afternoon. Who's living in that caravan up on the moor behind Venton's place?"

He rapped out the last question so quickly that the three children were too surprised to answer it. Mary was the first to recover her wits and she said coldly, "The caravan belongs to Mr Sparrow. Thank you for the drink. Good morning."—and they walked away.

They met Jon and David half-way up the hill and told them what had happened.

"But we don't really know much more about him," Mary admitted. "He must be staying at the inn because he took his big leather case in there. He wouldn't tell us what was in that case, and was touchy about it, if you know what I mean. And he asked about cellars again. Why does he want to know if Mr Sparrow has got a cellar?"

"He's got a bomb in the leather case and he wants to put it in our cellar and blow us all up," Dickie suggested. "I wish he'd blow himself up."

They told Mr Sparrow what little they had found out at lunch and the old man was very amused by their descriptions of the interview. He seemed to have recovered his spirits and suggested that the twins and Harriet should go out for the afternoon. He gave them enough money to go to Whitby on the bus from Goathland and to have their tea out.

Soon after they had gone, when Jon and David were being shown some of Mr Sparrow's treasures in the shop, the door opened and Warner came in.

"There is no need for you to go, boys," the old man said quietly. "Good afternoon, Mr Warner. I have considered your proposition most carefully and while I naturally thank you—or whoever you are representing—for so impressive an offer, I wish to make it clear now that I am not interested in selling this house, the business or the land. Nothing will persuade me to change my mind. Good afternoon."

The boys, who were watching Warner carefully, saw him go pale with anger. He opened his mouth to speak but Mr Sparrow opened the shop door for him.

"This place is my home, and here I intend to stay for the rest of my life. Good afternoon."

"And you're sure that nothing will make you change your mind?" Warner said in a shaking voice.

"I am positive. Good afternoon again."

Warner turned on his heel and David heard him mutter, "We'll soon see about that," as he went out.

Mr Sparrow refused to discuss the matter further and for the next hour he talked to them about glass and china and silver in so fascinating a way that they forgot the time and that it was fine outside. At last, when he got the chance, David told him that they had decided to sleep in their tents instead of the caravan while the weather was good, and that they were going up to the edge of the moor now to put up their camp.

As they walked up the track David admitted to Jon that he too was sure that they had met Warner before.

"There's something fishy going on here, Jon. That chap Warner is no good, I'm sure. I heard him threaten old Sparrow when he went out. What is it the old man has got that somebody wants to buy from him?"

Jon shook his head.

"I've got some ideas, David, but they're so crazy that I don't want to say much yet. Before we put up the tents, let's go and look at the mine. I'd like to go down there. Wonder how we could manage it?"

They found their answer much more quickly than they had expected, for as they breasted the rise just beyond the caravan they saw a man disappearing over the parapet surrounding the shaft. They saw him only as his head vanished but both had the impression that he had a bundle on his back.

"See him, David? I bet that's Warner! Let's go down there after him, using his ladder. If it will bear him it will take us one at a time. This is our chance to see what he's doing."

"So it is, Jon, but there's no hurry. Give him time to get down. There's a torch in the caravan and we'd better put on our sweaters and thick shoes. Wish we knew the depth of the shaft."

Jon, more excited than David had ever seen him, ran back to the caravan. There was only one torch—a big one cased in rubber—and as they struggled into more suitable clothes David had the ridiculous thought that they had nothing with which to defend themselves. He was suspicious about Warner and as they trotted up to the shaft he said, "There's no need to give ourselves away to Warner—or whoever it is. Let's just try and find out what's happening down there and keep out of his way."

Jon agreed. "All the same, we're looking after old Sparrow's interests. It's his land and his mine and that man is a trespasser . . . Here we are. Better not talk. I'll go first with the torch and you follow when I shake the ladder."

They tested the steel hooks holding the nylon ladder to the stone wall, and looked down into the darkness. There was nothing to see and nothing to hear but the drip of water.

"Quiet as you can," David whispered. "Don't give us away, Jon. If he's anywhere near the bottom of the shaft or you see a light you'd better come up again. I shall know when you're down because the ladder will go slack."

Jon nodded, climbed over the parapet, and David saw the hooks take the strain as his friend's head disappeared into the darkness. No sound came from below. Then the ladder shook and as David peered down into the depths he saw a flicker of light like a tiny welcoming star. Jon must have flashed the torch to show him that all was well.

As he climbed over the parapet David felt his heart thudding with excitement, and his mouth was dry as his feet found the soft "rungs" of the ladder and his hands grasped the twisted nylon. He began to go down. It was most unpleasant. Twice he scraped his knuckles on the rough stones and once banged his head. Step by step and hand over hand. He looked up and saw that the circle of daylight above him was now no bigger than a fat, full moon. Darkness closed round him and he could no longer see. His arms ached and he longed to feel something solid under his feet.

Suddenly the ladder went taut and through the darkness came a hoarse whisper.

"O.K., David. You're nearly down. I've got the ladder."

A few more steps and he stepped into soft, sticky mud.

"I can't hear him, but he can't be very far away," Jon whispered. "I've had a quick look round with the torch and there's a gallery running slightly downhill about twenty yards to the right. There's a lot of water about, and I should think we're standing in the same mud that Warner had on his boots. I've seen his footsteps. There's quite a lot of them so I should think he's been here before."

David rubbed his cold hands together and nodded in the dark.

"The air's fresh enough, Jon. Let's do as you say and try the gallery if that's the way he went, but keep quiet so that we can hear him coming. Switch on the torch for a sec."

The welcome beam swept round the big, artificial cave and stopped at the entrance to the gallery. Minerals sparkled on the walls as the light passed over them. Then Jon, with the beam focused on the ground a yard ahead of them, led the way into the gallery which, as he said, sloped down quite sharply into the heart of the moor. The walls were damp and in some places there had been falls of earth and stones over which they had to step carefully. Suddenly the gallery swung sharply to the left, and as they turned the corner they heard an odd sound echoing along the gallery towards them. "Footsteps," Jon whispered as he switched off the torch. "He's coming back," and even as he spoke they saw a glow of light ahead of them.

"Get back to the shaft," David urged. "We dare not meet him here . . . Might get up the ladder first and wait for him at the top . . . Give me the torch now and I'll lead."

Jon passed it over and they groped their way back towards the turn in the passage. Once round the corner David was prepared to use their light and run for it. Above their heavy breathing they could hear the shuffling footsteps of the man coming up behind them. He seemed to sense that something was wrong for he was coming fast.

They reached the corner. As they rounded it, David switched on the torch and suddenly stumbled on a loose stone. With a cry of alarm he fell forward on his face and the torch, still alight, slipped from his hand and rolled away from him.

He heard Jon's grunt of surprise, but as he tried to struggle to his feet the footsteps behind them broke into a run.

5. Hatchholt

HIGH IN THE Shropshire hills, at the head of one of the narrow valleys which split the eastern escarpment of the curiously shaped mountain known as the Long Mynd, is a reservoir. Two hundred yards below the stone wall which dams the water is a small, neat cottage tucked into the hill-side and sheltered from the westerly gales which come tearing over the Mynd from Wales. The pipe-line from the reservoir runs down this valley which is called Hatchholt, and a telephone wire links the cottage with the outside world. The nearest village, which is on the railway line between Shrewsbury and Hereford, is Onnybrook. The nearest house, which can only be reached by footpath, is over the hills flanking the southern side of the Hatchholt valley. It is called Witchend and belongs to the Morton family.

In the Hatchholt cottage lives Mr Jasper Sterling in retirement. He loves the hills and their solitude, but life starts afresh for him at the beginning of each holiday when his only daughter Petronella comes home from school in Shrewsbury.

On the morning of the third day after the events described in the last chapter, Mr Sterling, Peter and Penny Warrender were sitting down to breakfast in the kitchen of Hatchholt.

"There you are, Penelope," Mr Sterling said as he passed her a plate of bacon and egg. "Do you like your bacon curly at the edges?"

Penny flashed him a smile.

"I like bacon practically any way, Mr Sterling. Thank you so much. And thank you again for letting me come and stay with Peter. I love your house and the hills and it's wonderful to be here again . . . And I think you're a darling to cook and serve our breakfast."

The old man's eyes twinkled at her. How nice these two girls looked, and yet so different in character and appearance and undoubtedly very good for each other. Mr Sterling's heart warmed as he glanced at his daughter's gleaming fair head and when she looked up and saw him regarding her she gave him an affectionate smile in return.

"What shall we do this morning, Peter?" asked Penny.

"We might go over to the farm presently and see Tom and Mr and Mrs Ingles," Peter replied cheerfully. "First of all, though, we'll saddle Sally and go down the valley and collect the post and the paper for Dad."

Penny had forgotten that the postman never came to the cottage, but left the mail in a box nailed to a gate-post a mile or more down the pipe-line.

So after the girls had washed up and made their beds, Peter saddled her Welsh pony Sally and they went down the valley together.

Before they had gone very far Penny said, "I didn't say much last night, Peter, because I was tired and it was so wonderful to be here, but aren't you mad with David and Jon for going off on their own to Yorkshire? I was absolutely livid."

Peter laughed. "I bet you were . . . I don't think I mind much, Penny. It's turned out all right, hasn't it? You're here, and maybe we'll soon see Tom and Jenny and I wouldn't be surprised if we don't see the others too before the end of the holidays. We could go off somewhere on our own if we want to, couldn't we?"

"Of course we could. That's what makes me so mad. Those two boys never even seem to consider that we might. Of course, later I pretended that I didn't care where they went or for how long they stayed wherever they were going. I was quite charming to them when I said 'Good-bye' and *so* polite, Peter. It was rather fun, really. Mrs Morton was sweet to me, of course, and I had one or two good days in London with her, and then she suggested that

I telephone you and my aunt in Rye and here we are."

They changed the subject and talked about school until they reached the post-box. There were four letters—three for Mr Sterling and a fat one with a Yorkshire postmark for Peter who blushed a little when she recognized the writing.

"It's from David," she said, unnecessarily. "Funny we were just talking about them."

"Not funny," Penny said. "Would you like me to fade away while you read it? Of course, Jon doesn't know I'm here. I didn't tell him. I s'pose he thinks I'm still pining for him at Brownlow Square. All boys are utterly selfish."

Peter stuffed all the letters in the pocket of her jodhpurs and remounted Sally.

"So they are, Penny. I like boys, though. One or two, anyway. Let's go back to the cottage and give Dad his mail and the paper, and then we'll go up to the reservoir and see what David's got to say."

Penny agreed good-humouredly and half an hour later they were lying in a sunny hollow just above the water.

"Just read out the unprivate bits," Penny said as Peter slit the envelope. It was a long letter and she looked pleased with herself as she read the first two pages silently. "Those were sort of private," she said, with an apologetic look at her friend. "They're all right and have joined up with the others at this village Spaunton. But listen, Penny. They seem to have got mixed up with an adventure which concerns Mr Sparrow . . . Come here and read it with me."

Once having settled down to write a letter, David did not spare himself, and Penny was a little envious of his obvious ability. He wrote well and amusingly of their trek across the moor in the fog and of everything that had happened to them since. When they got to the dramatic story of their descent into the mine Penny, in her excitement, grabbed the sheet on which it was written and tore it.

"You're breathing down my neck," Peter said indignantly. "And it is my letter anyway. Just sit back and I'll read the rest to you."

"*Go on!*" Penny hissed. "I just got to where David fell

down and they heard the shuffling footsteps coming nearer and nearer. *Do go on, Peter.*"

Peter sat up and began to read.

"There was I grovelling about on the slimy floor of the gallery with the torch out of reach and the enemy coming up behind us. Jon helped me up and we were groping for the torch when the chap came round the corner and blundered into us. He had one of those big electric lamps and we were dazzled by the beam which shone into our faces. We could not see him but he recognized us at once, and we knew that it was Warner as soon as he began to swear at us. Anyway, he blustered and told us to get out and that we were trespassing. This annoyed Jon very much—me too—and he told Warner straight out that *he* was the trespasser because the mine was on old Sparrow's land and belonged to him, and that if he did not shut up and get out we would report him to the police. Then he asked how we got down and when we told him by his ladder he nearly had a fit! I told him that we had more right down there than he had, and that we were interested in old mines and that now we had found our way down we should certainly come again. At that he changed his tune and said, 'No use arguing down here. You two get on ahead and use your torch. I'll have more to say when we get to the top.' Anyway, we went on ahead and he followed. We weren't able to see him until we got to the foot of the shaft and there was room to turn round. He'd got a knapsack on his back and a squarish leather case round his neck. This was big and looked heavy. Jon walked over to the ladder and tested it. Then he said, 'We'll go up first, Mr Warner. Like me to carry that heavy case for you?'

" 'Certainly not,' he snapped. 'Mind your own business and get up as quickly as you can. One at a time.'

"I nodded to Jon and he passed me the torch and started up the ladder. I could just see a tiny circle of light far away at the top of the shaft and I kept a tight hold on the bottom of the ladder. I was not very keen on being alone down there with Warner and had a silly idea that he might go for me, climb up after Jon and then pull the ladder up. I did not say anything and after a bit he tried to be friendly and said that he was a geologist and interested in mines and caves. He told us that he had come out of our mine in a hurry because it was very dangerous and that the roof of the gallery had fallen farther along. I did not really believe him. He was too anxious to warn us off. Anyway, after what seemed an hour but was not, the ladder went slack and then shook so I knew that Jon was safely up. Before Warner could say anything I started to climb up and I do not want to do it again. It was really hard work and I had had about enough when Jon helped me over the parapet and we flopped down together on the grass. It was good to be out of that place. We waited for Warner to come up and he looked as if he had had enough too. He sat down with his back to the wall but he kept his hands on the big leather case. When he had got his breath back he hauled up the ladder. It rolled up into a fairly small bundle and he put it in the rucksack and then he took a good look at us and said, 'Take my advice and keep out of that place. I've been in there farther than you and it's very dangerous. Keep out.'

"Before I could say my piece, Jon got up and said his.

" 'That's all right, Mr Warner. Thanks for warning us, but we shall tell Mr Sparrow about this. You're trespassing and if we see you up here on his land we'll tell the police. The old fence shows the boundary. All the land from the fence down to the house is private and you'd better go back another way.'

"He went off muttering and cursing and Jon said what I was thinking. 'Wish I knew what he's got in that leather case?'

"I haven't a clue as to what he's up to but I believe Jon has. You know what he is! He won't say anything until he's sure.

"There's one more thing to tell you about before I come to the really important reason for this letter. I told you at the beginning that old man Sparrow is well enough looked after by a slightly crazy woman called Miss Wildblood who lives in a tiny cottage on the opposite side of the village street. Last night after supper Grandpa Sparrow sent Harriet over to give her a message. When she came back she was almost too excited to speak, but eventually she told us that she knocked on the cottage door and as usual walked straight in. The Wildblood was in there talking to Warner.

"You're now up to date with our news. I explained why Jon and I thought we'd like to go away for a hike together, but we must stay here now. You can see, Peter, that we're almost right in another adventure. There's more than one person trying to get Mr Sparrow out of his place and it's all to do with the mine. Warner has got something to do with it, and I'm now as sure as the twins that we've run across him before, but I can't place him. We must back up Mr Sparrow who, although determined not to be bribed out of Yorkshire, is rather shaken and talking of going back to London to discuss the peculiar goings on with Mr Venton. We're all determined to get this sorted out.

"We can't have an adventure without you, Peter and we all want you to come here as soon as you can. We'd like Tom and Jenny if they could manage it, and Jon has written to Penny who is still at Brownlow Square—"

"Stop!" Penny shouted. "Stop, Peter! They think I'm in London moping for them! Ha! Ha! Mr Warrender! Maybe he'll ring up the Mortons and I won't be there. This is what Dickie calls fabulous . . . You can go on now."

Peter giggled and read the rest of the letter.

"Jon has written to Penny because of course we want her too. There's a grand caravan up on the edge of the moor for you two to sleep in and Jon and I have got our tents.

"Please come, Peter, but tell your father how sorry we are to take you away. The twins and Harriet send their love. I'll telephone Hatchholt after seven to have your answer. We want you and Penny and we'll manage to put the others up if they can manage it, but I leave that to you."

Peter folded the letter and put it back in her pocket.

"That's all. We'll go, won't we, Penny? We must go. Dad won't mind. I told you it would all work out properly and you see how much they want us. Let's go back to the cottage and tell Dad and then we'll go over to Ingles and ask Tom if he can come and we must telephone Jenny too."

And so the Lone Piners were gradually being united again. Mr Sterling and Penny's aunt were agreeable but Tom and Jenny were both needed on the farm and in the shop. Late that afternoon the girls started to make their preparations and they were just finishing their packing when the telephone rang. Peter rushed to answer it as Penny hissed, "Don't let him know I'm here. Just speak for yourself."

"Yes, David, it's me. Yes, I got your letter. Yes, I can come tomorrow. The best station is Whitby, you say, and I must come via York. What's that? Jon wants to speak to me? All right. I'm still here."

She held the receiver away from her ear and whispered to Penny, "Jon wants to speak to *me*. What shall I say if he asks me about you?"

A crackling noise came from the receiver, so Penny put her head against Peter's and heard Jon's deep voice say, "Hello, Peter. Glad you can come. Tell Penny we're all looking forward to seeing her. See you both at Whitby station tomorrow evening. Cheerio!"

Then he rang off. Peter replaced their receiver and began to laugh. Penny gave up the struggle of pretending to be offended and flopped into a chair.

"He makes me so *mad*, Peter. He's so superior, but what a fool I was. Of course he telephoned to Mrs Morton who told him I was with you, and here was I thinking he'd be fed up because he wouldn't know where I was. Never mind. Just for once I don't mind being a good girl and doing what I'm told."

6. *Goathland*

THE MOORLAND VILLAGE of Goathland in the North Riding of Yorkshire is a favourite place for holiday-makers. Sheep graze on the grass verges of the wide street and in the summer nearly every house and cottage takes in visitors. But although Goathland is small, it has a railway station and this double-track line is a remarkable example of railway engineering planned by the great George Stephenson.

Two days after Peter and Penny had received their telephone message from Yorkshire, half a dozen people were waiting on the sunny platform of Goathland station for the train to Whitby. Five of the waiting passengers were laughing and talking together when the little train came in, but the sixth remained lounging on the seat with his legs outstretched. The others crowded into one compartment and the guard called:

"Coming aboard, sir?"

"No, I am not."

The man on the seat was Warner and he looked grubbier and untidier than usual. As the guard waved his flag, Warner showed no surprise when he saw a stoutish man in a tweed suit and fisherman's hat walking along the platform towards him. He was the "Doctor" in yet another disguise.

He sat down next to Warner and neither spoke until the train was out of sight.

"I want to say that I consider this to be a ridiculous place to meet," Warner said quietly. "And the signalman is watching us."

"He's only watching two holiday-makers who have decided to wait here for the next train," the "Doctor" said. "Now, Robbie. Your report, please. I assume by your cocksure manner that you have good news."

"You're right. I've done what you asked me. There is no question that there are deposits of uranium in the old mine working at Spaunton. It has been hard and dangerous work to get the evidence, but I have a rough record in my pocket and I have no doubt. The detector you sent me is admirable."

The "Doctor's" eyes gleamed triumphantly.

"Well done, Robbie. I thought Spaunton would be fruitful. Let me see your records."

Warner handed over a paper covered with figures and diagrams of the mine workings.

"So far, so good," the "Doctor" said as he pocketed the paper. "If our colleagues who are covering the rest of the North Country are half as fortunate as you have been, Robbie, we are all going to make a lot of money. We shall be able to buy up any private land where there are uranium deposits, and provided the owner has no suspicion of its value we can re-sell to the Atomic Energy Authority at a very handsome profit. If all goes well you are not going to have any more financial worries . . . Now to business. All these deals must be rushed through before the owners grasp what is happening. The Spaunton mine belongs to the man who bought Venton's, does it not? What is his name?"

"Name of Sparrow, believe it or not. He's only just bought the place and he comes from London. He's proving difficult."

"My dear Robbie! No small difficulties must be allowed to stand in our way now. I remember taking a chance on that mine when we heard Venton had decided to sell out. I was confident of Spaunton but Venton didn't seem interested. Odd. Can't understand it. Now what about Sparrow?"

Warner looked sulky.

"I've made the old fool two very handsome offers within the limits you set me but he won't listen."

"*Won't* listen? This is nonsense, Robbie. What do you mean he won't listen? Doesn't he want money?"

"Don't think he does. Just not interested. Keeps the shop

as a sort of hobby and talks a lot of nonsense about wanting to spend the rest of his days here on the moors."

"He *must* be interested, Robbie. We'll increase the offer but he must be got out quickly. We want possession of the house, the garden and all the land. It's worth nearly any money to get him out. We must be the legitimate owners of the whole property in a few weeks. What are you finding so difficult? It's only a matter of perseverance and salesmanship on your part and plenty of money. We're playing for a big prize, Robbie. Old man Sparrow must be got out for good and there's no time to waste. What's the trouble?"

"Nothing specific except that he's stubborn. After my last try with him he got one of the locals to board over the mine shaft, but that doesn't matter so much because there's no need for me to go down again at present . . It's odd, Doctor, but I've a hunch that there might be an entrance into the old mine workings through the cellar. The garden slopes down steeply to the back of the house."

"We'll see about that when we get possession of the place, Robbie. Nothing to worry about if he's closed up the entrance to the shaft. Just as well to keep other people out. We don't want anyone else poking their noses into our mine. You say he's stubborn, but there are more ways of getting a stubborn man to change his mind than money. He's living there alone, isn't he?"

Warner got up and walked to the edge of the platform.

"No he isn't," he said over his shoulder. "He's got a lot of kids staying there. They make it more difficult because they're always about the place. The old man has got a granddaughter in the house. There are also twins and there's something about those two that worries me. I'm sure I've seen them before somewhere."

"Come back here and sit down, Robbie," the "Doctor" said softly. "That's right! I don't think you can be feeling well. What is all this nonsense about children getting in the way, and twins you have seen before?"

"I tell you the place is littered with kids," Warner snapped. "Don't talk as if I was an idiot. I'm doing the work there and not you, and I tell you that these kids are much too curious. Besides those three youngsters, there are two lads of about sixteen who are now camping a few yards from the mine shaft, and two girls about the same age sleeping in a caravan on the edge of the moor. They're a nuisance. They're suspicious and I've got the feeling that one or other of them is always watching me."

He did not mention that Jon and David had followed him down into the mine, feeling that he would not be very popular if he did! Before the "Doctor" could comment, Warner went on quickly:

"Anyway, I've made arrangements to watch the Sparrow outfit very carefully. The old man has taken on a woman called Wildblood as daily housekeeper. She lives in a cottage on the other side of the street and used to work for Venton."

"What name did you say? The woman's?"

"Wildblood. Sounds odd, but she looks wild and will do anything for money. I've fixed that. She tells me what they talk about in the house and what they do."

"How much have you told her, Robbie? Does she know what we're after? You say 'No', but you can't be sure. I don't like the way you're handling this, Robbie. You're getting soft and I'm going to take over. Leave Spaunton and go back to Whitby and wait until I let you know time and place of our next meeting. Clear out of that pub without any fuss but keep in touch with the Wildblood woman. Get her to write to you—if she can write. And don't believe everything she tells you because she may be making up stories just to get money. Just keep her sweet because she may be useful to us in other ways."

Warner nodded. "You won't be any luckier with Sparrow than I've been. I know him. You've never met him and I tell you he won't sell."

"I think he will. If he can't be bought with money, I shall persuade him, one way or another, to quit. You have not been as smart as I hoped, Robbie. I never thought to hear you make a pack of children an excuse for failure."

Warner fumbled for another cigarette, but before he could light it the two men heard a dog bark and looked up to see a lively black Scottie watching them with his head on one side from the opposite platform. He was followed by twins and two older, pretty girls.

Warner laughed but there was no humour in it.

"There you are, Doctor!" he whispered. "Here's a selection of the dear little innocent children from Venton's. How did they know we were here? They've followed me, of course. They're not as innocent as they look. We'd better clear out"—and he turned his back to the Lone Piners.

The "Doctor" frowned. "Those twins. You say you've seen them before Spaunton? I seem to remember them too . . . No, Robbie. Don't go. I'm going to handle this"—and he stood up and walked to the edge of the platform.

The four children regarded the two men gravely for a long half-minute and then Mary smiled and said:

"It's that nice Mr Warner, twin. So it is. Good afternoon, Mr Warner. Isn't it a lovely day for a walk? Thank you so much for that drink you gave us the other day . . . Peter and Penny—this is Mr Warner who has been staying at *The Yorkshire Rose*. He knows Grandpa Sparrow."

Before either of the girls could speak, the "Doctor" broke in.

"Good afternoon. Are you all waiting for the Pickering train? It should be due in ten minutes. Do you all live here, or, like me, are you visiting Yorkshire for the first time?"

"Acksherley we are," Mary replied. "Is Mr Warner your friend too? He's a very kind man but he is looking rather worried this afternoon."

"Don't talk about me as if I wasn't here," Warner snapped. "I've told you before that I don't like you. Clear out."

"We don't see why you should speak to us like that," Dickie said sulkily. "We saw you going for a walk after dinner, and we thought we'd like to go for a walk with our friends Peter and Penny. So out we came, and after a bit we saw you walking along the lane to Goathland, and we said we'd like to go to Goathland too so here we are."

"Oh, Mr Warner!" Mary went on. "We don't mean to be rude but how nice your clean shoes look! Generally you wear great big muddy boots, don't you?"

Warner spluttered and his face reddened as the "Doctor" put a hand on his arm.

"Come, my friend. Let us join these delightful children on the other platform. I am aware that I shall have to wait a long time here for a train to Pickering, shall I not, my dear?"—and he smiled across the rails at Penny.

Penny did not like being addressed as "my dear" by strangers, but she supposed she should make some response so she grinned feebly and said, "Yes, you will."

The "Doctor", still grasping Warner's arm, led him, rather as one leads a sleep-walker, down the platform to where they could cross the rails.

"Run and meet them, twins," Peter whispered. "Don't give them a chance to talk together privately"—and then, as Dickie and Mary ran off to meet the two men, Peter went on: "I don't like this, Penny. I'm just on the edge of remembering those two. The twins have been very, very smart."

As the men walked up the platform with their youthful attendants a bell clanged in the signal-box, and the signal at the end of the platform went down. The girls went to meet them. Warner was obviously baffled and furious while the "Doctor's" fixed smile was more obvious than sincere.

"So you're staying in Pickering?" Penny said to him. "Perhaps we shall have time to go there too. How nice to be keen on walking over these lovely moors."

"Where do you children live?" the "Doctor" asked with obvious effort. "I think you said you were all on holiday in Yorkshire?"

"We live in London," said Dickie.

"And I live in Sussex," said Penny.

"And I—" Peter began, and then changed her mind. "Never mind where I live! Are you going to Pickering now with your new friend, Mr Warner?"

Before he could answer, the train came in and they all crowded round to help the "Doctor" find a corner seat. When the door of the compartment was closed, and they were sure that Warner had not had a chance to exchange a private word with him, they stood back and waved and called "Good-bye!"

"Now wasn't that fun?" Mary suggested as the train disappeared round the curve on its way south.

"Wasn't it fun, Mr Warner? I mean us all meeting like that. Aren't you glad we came along and sort of brightened your afternoon."

"I am *never* glad to see any of you," Warner snapped. "Get out of my way. I've nothing more to say to you."

"Oh, but Mr Warner," Dickie pleaded. "Please don't go yet. There is something special we want to ask you. *Please, Mr Warner!* That nice man we've just been talking to. You didn't tell us his name. Have you ever met him before?"

"No, I have not," Warner snapped. "Never met him before. He just sat down next to me and got into conversation, if you must know. He's a keen walker."

"How perkewler," Mary said. "How very, very odd. Here's a nice old man all dressed up for walkin' or fishin' or something and all he does is to get out of one train, sit and talk to you and then go back by train and not do any walking at all."

"*And* while we're on the subject of walking," Dickie went on proudly, "there's another fabulous thing, Mr Warner. What a perkewler walk you've had. Fancy coming all the way from Spaunton for a walk just to have a nice sit down on Goathland station and a talk to somebody you didn't know."

Warner pushed him aside angrily.

"Get out of my way!" he shouted. "And if you want to keep out of trouble, don't follow me."

7. *The Second Stranger*

WHILE PETER, PENNY and the twins were at Goathland tormenting Warner and the stranger in the tweed fishing hat, the elder boys and Harriet soon became involved in another mystery.

Mr Sparrow told them that they could do what they liked as he intended to stay in for the rest of the day and look after the shop. David, much to Harriet's delight, said, "Come out with us, Harry. We'll go up to the moor."

They toiled up the track together and were out of breath when they reached the caravan. "Let's stop here and rest a minute," David suggested.

While he was speaking, Jon was standing on the steps of the caravan looking towards the mine shaft.

"Come a little farther up the hill," he said quietly. "Believe it or not there's somebody else messing about up there now. Surely it can't be Warner again?"

With a flash of temper Harriet said, "This place all belongs to us—or to my grandfather. *Why can't people let us alone?*"

David put a hand on her shoulder.

"Are you coming with us or going to stay in the caravan? If it's Warner I think we might get a little rough with him."

She smiled up at him.

"I'm so angry I'm shaking inside," she whispered. "Come on. I want to be with you."

Jon strode ahead but waited for them on the brow of the hill.

"It's not Warner," he said. "Just a second stranger if you count Warner the first. Looks a cool customer to me."

A man was sitting on the stone coping of the shaft watching them. He was young and pleasant-looking and his fair hair gleamed in the sunshine. On the ground was a well-stuffed rucksack and on the wall beside him a half-open map.

"Good afternoon," he said cheerfully. "Can you tell me whether the village below there is Spaunton?"

"Yes it is," David said. "And you're trespassing. This land belongs to Mr Sparrow and he's tired of strangers tramping over his property. His boundary is where the old wire fence has broken down. It's quite clear."

The young man looked surprised and faintly amused.

"It isn't very clear, you know. Only one or two posts of the fence are standing and there's not much chance of seeing any of the old wire. Anyway, I'm doing no harm and I don't think Mr Sparrow would mind me. Who are you, anyway? Aren't you trespassing too?"

"We're not trespassing, but you are," Harriet said quietly. "Mr Sparrow is my grandfather and these two boys are our friends and they're staying with us. Will you please go."

"I don't think I will," the stranger smiled. "If your grandfather lives here, I would like to talk to him." He turned to David. "Did you say that Mr Sparrow is bothered by strangers on his property? Is that why he has just covered over the shaft of the old Spaunton mine? The timber and barbed wire look very new. Is the mine dangerous now?"

David flushed with annoyance because he knew that he was not getting the better of this argument.

"You're asking a lot of questions. Although you don't seem to care, you're still trespassing and we must ask you to go."

The stranger smiled again and began to fill his pipe.

"I'll go if you'll take me to see Mr Sparrow. I promise that he won't mind me. My name is Sharman—Philip Sharman. I'm a geologist and I live in York. I'm interested in old mines and I like exploring them. There are several deserted mines in this county and I found two beauties last summer in Swaledale. Any of you ever been there?"

Harriet smiled at him and he was now fairly sure that they were on his side. Jon was not won over so easily and said:

"No, we haven't been there, but you haven't explained why you're so keen about mines. Is there anything special about this one?"

"All mines have something special about them. Spaunton is marked on the one-inch map and I'd like to go down if I could and perhaps one of you chaps would like to come too. Mr Sparrow must know whether it's safe or not, so let's ask him. I assure you that I'm quite harmless." He turned to Harriet and added, specially for her benefit. "You trust me, don't you? What did you say your name was?"

She told him and rather grudgingly the boys introduced themselves and together they went down to the house. Sharman laughed and joked with them. He also asked a lot of questions, the answers to which the boys skilfully avoided. Just before they reached the garden David asked Harriet to run ahead and tell her grandfather that they were bringing somebody to see him. When Harriet had gone, Sharman changed his tone and said seriously, "I can't think why you don't trust me. Have you been having trouble up here?"

"We're camping up there, and we don't like strangers," David said evasively. "Mr Sparrow is very nice but he's funny about trespassers."

Sharman looked at them quizzically and then, as they turned into the village street, he stopped to glance at Venton's shop window.

"This is Mr Sparrow's shop," Jon explained.

Within five minutes Philip Sharman had won over Mr Sparrow, who discovered that he was interested in old glass and china and knew a lot about antique furniture. After a while the boys and Harriet got bored with all this talk and wandered out into the street.

"What did you tell your grandfather about him, Harry?" David asked. "Before we came in, I mean?"

"Just that he was sitting on the mine shaft and was crazy about mines and I didn't think you two liked him. I like him though. He's very, very handsome . . ." she added unexpectedly and blushed when the boys laughed at her.

"Too many people are interested in this place," David

said. "I wish the others would come back. We're being feeble and just mooching about. Let's go up to the moor again and leave Mr Sharman to your grandfather. Come on."

Mr Sparrow saw them as they passed the shop window and called them in.

"Mr Sharman is on a tramping holiday, and we have so much in common that I have asked him to stay to tea with us. Please put the kettle on Harriet. No, no . . . We shall be delighted to have your company, and my young people would like to hear something more about the archaelogical and geological treasures of Yorkshire."

Jon and David glanced at each other in surprise. What were they in for now? However, there was nothing they could do because Mr Sparrow had undoubtedly accepted Sharman without suspicion, and when the two men came into the sitting-room ten minutes later the latter had a parcel under his arm which he put with great care on the window-ledge.

David thought that he winked at him as he said:

"I've been very lucky, David. First to meet you chaps and so have a chance of meeting Mr Sparrow and picking his brains about my hobby, and secondly of buying from him four coffee-cups at a bargain price."

Harriet, who had heard her grandfather selling something before now, doubted very much whether Sharman was right, but she had the wisdom to say nothing and passed round the scones. David and Jon munched through an uneasy silence which was broken by Sharman who began to talk to them about Yorkshire. He told them many strange tales and legends of ancient days and old superstitions.

Harriet was listening eagerly when he passed his cup for more tea.

"You like old things as much as your grandfather, don't you, Harriet? If I decide to stay for a few days round these parts, would you like me to show you some old places? Good! We'll see what I have time for, but did you know about the Roman road which is only about two miles from here?"

"We saw it on the map," David said. "What's it like?"

"It's a rough road, but it's there for you to walk on for more than a mile. It's on Wheeldale Moor and the actual stones are still there—some of them too big for a vehicle to drive over now without being shaken to pieces, but they're not covered with weeds or grass. This stretch of road has been cared for since the war and I don't think you'll see anything else like it in Britain. You can walk where the legions marched, Harriet."

"I'd like to do that. Tell us some more," she said.

"I think I can do better than a Roman road if it's a thrill you want. Did you know that there is what we can justly call a forgotten village not many miles farther from here than the Roman road?"

Mr Sparrow looked up in surprise.

"You mean Coram Street, Mr Sharman? I have heard of it but never been there. Have you been excavating there?"

Sharman nodded.

"Indeed we have. I like some archaeology sometimes. A lot of work was done there last summer, and a few of us will probably be there each fine week-end soon."

"But how is it forgotten?" Harriet pleaded. "Tell us about it."

"It would take you a long time to find Coram Street by yourselves. No roads lead to it now. There's only a sunken track made by wagon wheels hundreds of years ago and it runs from a lane, over the fields to a valley. It's odd that through this valley runs a single-line railway track, but that too is in danger of being forgotten, for the line is now closed. On the opposite side of the valley are the buried foundations of an ancient village and manor-house. We are working on these and I will show them to you if you are interested."

"I'd like to see it," Jon said quickly. "I don't much care for monuments and old things but your forgotten village sounds intriguing. Why has it been forgotten? Why doesn't anybody live there now?"

"What we shall be working on in a few weeks' time are the foundations of dwellings many hundreds of years old.

The Black Death in the fourteenth century wiped out the populations of many villages like Coram Street."

"Sounds very ghostly," Harriet whispered. "Hasn't anybody else ever lived there?"

"Not on the hill, but in the valley there are a few ruined cottages. There's a decaying church, too—nasty place. I hate churches which aren't used for their proper purpose. I think the devil gets in, don't you?"

They looked at him in surprise and Mr Sparrow said, "You could be right, Mr Sharman. Continue if you please."

"You can still see a well-defined track leading down the shoulder of the hill to the church and this is correctly called a Corpse Way. Along this path in all weathers the bodies of those who died in near-by villages without a church were carried in coffins by bearers to Coram Street for burial. It isn't a very cheerful place and I don't think anyone lives there now. The railway runs into a tunnel to the north, and I believe there are some ruined cottages at the other end where there used to be a big quarry. Anyway, it's not often you have the chance of seeing a place like Coram Street, so I'll show it to you one day if I'm around and you're still here."

They were all impressed by his description of the forgotten village and sat in silence for a few moments. Then, because the door between the shop and the living-room was open, they suddenly heard a dog bark in the street and then the sound of joyful and familiar voices.

David jumped up. "Excuse me. That sounds as if the twins are up to something"—and he ran out into the street.

He was right. The twins were in action. About fifteen yards ahead of them, and now almost on the brow of the hill leading down to *The Yorkshire Rose*, the man calling himself Warner was in full retreat. There was no doubt that he was very angry because he turned and shook both clenched fists at the twins who, with an excited Mackie were hopping and skipping down the middle of the street. They were followed, about fifteen yards in the rear, by Peter and Penny, who were looking embarrassed as some of the villagers came to their front doors to see the cause of the commotion.

"Oh, Mr Warner . . ." Mary was chanting. "Dear Mr Warner, please don't run away. *Please don't run away.* Our legs are so small that we can't keep up with you."

Then Dickie saw the others at the shop door and waved cheerfully.

"Shan't be long!" he called. "We're hungry and exhausted but we think p'raps our nice Mr Warner is going to give us some tea at the inn . . . *Please don't shout like that, Mr Warner.* We can't hear you when you shout."

"We're ashamed to be with them," Penny said as she and Peter came up, although her mouth was twitching. "I'm almost sorry for Warner. Let's go indoors because we've a lot to tell you. Don't worry about the twins. Nobody will be able to stop them now."

"Yes, let them go, David," Peter said excitedly. "I know they're worse than usual, but they're making him so mad that he may do something very silly . . . We've got some terrific news, David. I know who that chap is"—and having got as far as that, she cried out as David gripped her wrist.

"Not now," he whispered.

She turned and saw Mr Sparrow, with a good-looking young man, standing in the shop doorway. Peter coloured as she caught the man's eye because she had the feeling that he had heard what she had been saying. Mr Sparrow then introduced the girls to Philip Sharman who followed them back into the sitting-room.

Peter and Penny settled down to their tea, but as neither Mr Sparrow nor Sharman seemed disposed to go elsewhere, they had to wait to tell their story to the boys.

"Are you on a walking holiday too, Mr Sharman?" Penny asked. "We haven't been here very long but we keep on meeting walkers. Do you collect things?"

Sharman looked at her coolly until she blushed.

"I collect both information and specimens," he said. "When I have gone on my way, no doubt your friends will tell you about our first meeting and of Mr Sparrow's hospitality to a stranger . . . I have one further favour to ask you, sir. I have told you that geology is my subject and I want to ask you to allow me to explore the old mine, although I see that you have recently covered up the shaft. I'm not inexperienced in this sort of work, and my real purpose in coming to Spaunton is to take a look at your mine. I have all the equipment I need, and I hope you will give me permission to go down. I'll put the covers back, of course."

The boys exchanged a meaning glance, but before either of them could speak, Mr Sparrow said sharply, "I'm sorry, Mr Sharman, but I cannot permit that. The mine shaft has been closed because it is dangerous. Moreover it is on my land and I consider myself responsible. Whatever your interests, I am afraid that I must forbid you to go down into the Spaunton mine."

Mr Sharman stood up and smiled.

"I cannot press you, sir, but Spaunton mine should be of particular interest. I have always believed that it could have more than one entrance, and now that I have seen its position for myself, I am wondering whether there might not be a tunnel coming out by the river in the valley below—or even in the basement of this house if you have a cellar. If any of you youngsters ever find another entrance to the mine I hope you'll let me know."

"Where shall we find you, Mr Sharman?" Jon asked quickly. "We like the idea of looking for hidden tunnels."

Sharman laughed. "I'll keep in touch, and thank you very much for my tea. I shall see you all again, soon I hope. Perhaps I'll take some of you to the deserted village one day soon. Goodbye and thank you again"—and he picked up the parcel of coffee-cups he had bought and went out with Mr Sparrow.

As the door closed behind the two men, the others all began to talk until David silenced them.

"Do shut up, please! Peter's got something important to tell us, but don't let's discuss *anything* with Mr Sparrow yet. We'll have to tell him everything soon, Harriet, but we must talk it over together first. I'm going to fetch the twins now, and let's all meet at the caravan in a quarter of an hour. Better bring some food for the twins else they'll want to come in here first."

Ten minutes later they were all in the caravan. The twins, who were tired and hungry after their escapade, ate chunks of bread and jam and fruit cake, while Peter began her story.

"First of all, Penny and twins, I'm sorry not to have told you about this until now, but I did think that I ought to wait because it's an important Club thing and it should be told to as many members as possible—"

"What about me?" Harriet interrupted. "I'm just a girl who does everything for your Club *except* be a member."

"You're in it, Harry," Penny said. "You can't escape now, but you can't actually sign your name in your own blood on what Dickie calls the 'dokkerment' until we take you to Witchend because that's where it's hidden. We'll take you soon. We all think you're a member, don't we, David?"

David nodded and nodded to Peter to go on with her story while Harriet beamed at them all enthusiastically.

"I can't think why neither the twins nor David spotted this man. When we last met him he called himself John Robens. Don't you remember our adventure with him? He was living in an old cottage called Greystone End and experimenting on dogs. He got hold of Mackie—"

A whoop of triumph came from the twins.

"That's it!" Dickie yelled. "Of course you're right, Peter, but he hadn't got a beard then."

"And darling Mackie was captured by him—and OF COURSE, Peter. He was the man who came after us in the cave, and in a way he rescued us, Peter, after you had fallen down into that horrible place."

Then David clapped his hand to his forehead.

"What a fool I am, Peter! Of course you're right. I'm not likely to forget that adventure* considering what you did, and yet I couldn't place this chap."

* *The Neglected Mountain*

"Let me get on, please," Peter pleaded. "I can't be sure why Robens is here now but you may remember—sorry you weren't with us then, Jon and Penny—that the Robens' adventure really started when that charter plane came down on the Long Mynd. There were two passengers in a great hurry to get somewhere and they came to Hatchholt and scared me. One was Robens and the other was a doctor, but this was easy for me, because the first time I saw Robens he had a beard, but he was clean-shaven when we met him later. The other man called himself a doctor and lived in a house called The Limes in—"

"In Shrewsbury!" Dickie shouted triumphantly. "We remember. We went in and said we'd got awful pains and we got into the house, and there was Robens almost as angry as he was just now when he's Warner . . . You're marvellous, Peter. No wonder we were worried 'cos we couldn't quite remember him."

"The point really is whether either of them remember us," Peter said soberly. "Those two are crooks and although Robens could have left us in that terrible cave and didn't, we know how cruel and wicked he can be."

Here Jon interrupted and begged them to start from the beginning, because they seemed to forget that Penny and he had not been with them. He remembered now that David had once told him that Peter had, during this adventure in the caves in the Stiperstones, deliberately risked her own life in order to save Mary's. So they told Jon and Penny all they knew of the two accomplices, reminding each other that the "Doctor" had always been the leader.

"You're suspicious about what is going on here, aren't you, Jon?" David said. "I know you are. It's something to do with the mine, isn't it?"

"It must be the mine, of course," Jon agreed. "I think Mr Sparrow is being urged to sell Venton's because there are valuable mineral desposits either in the old mine or in this land. I read something in one of the papers about this a few weeks ago, but I can't be sure until I've been to a Public Library and checked on the file. As soon as I'm sure, I'll tell you."

Penny was furious.

"Don't be so stuffy and stuck-up, Jon! Just tell us now what you suspect instead of treating us like babies. You're afraid that you make yourself look a fool, I suppose? Please tell us."

"Sorry, but I won't say until I'm sure. It's too serious. I'll go to Whitby directly after breakfast and look in the Library. You can come with me, Penny, and then you'll be the first to know what a fool I am!"

"Oh, all right, Jon. I'd like to come, but I wish you wouldn't be so secretive—Harriet! Whatever is the matter?"

"It's something I've just remembered and something we all seem to have forgotten. Now we know that Warner really is an enemy, do you realize that he knows Miss Wildblood? I told you that he was talking to her in her cottage the other evening. I don't know what they were saying, but do you think they were plotting something together against Grandfather?"

"You mean that the Wildblood is a real traitor?" Dickie hissed. "If she is, that's absolutely monstrous, Harry."

"She's a witch," Mary said. "I bet she's got lots of broomsticks in her cottage and does spells. Shall we ask her, David?"

"You'll do nothing of the sort, but we must be careful what we say when she's in the room or could be listening. I suggest that tomorrow, as soon as Jon has done his checking-up in Whitby, we decide whether Mr Sparrow has got to be told everything we know. After all, the mine shaft is boarded over and Jon and I are on guard there at night. The girls are safe in the caravan, and the twins, Harry and Mackie, can guard the house at night. Let's not fuss Mr Sparrow any more today, but before supper I'd like to know whether Warner is still at *The Yorkshire Rose* and if he is, we must try to find out more about him. Will you walk down with me, Peter?"

"Of course, David. I agree that we shouldn't worry Mr Sparrow until we're more certain of what's really happening, but seeing Robens and the "Doctor" together again has scared me. I wonder if they recognized us? I bet they're worried about the twins."

"They nearly remembered us, I think," Mary suggested. "The 'Doctor' asked us where we lived."

"I nearly told him I lived in Shropshire and only just remembered in time," Peter said. "I think if I had given that away, he would have remembered seeing me at Hatchholt. It's the 'Doctor' I'm afraid of. Robens only does what he's told. Let's go down now and see whether he's at the inn."

"It would be better if Jon and I went," Penny suggested. "He hasn't seen us before. You two go for a walk somewhere else. And another thing. Do you all believe this young man Sharman with his tales about old mines and deserted villages? I don't. I think he's bogus too."

David laughed. "Find out all you can about Robens. We'll meet at the house for supper. Will your grandfather mind us exploring the cellar, Harriet? Good. And you two might keep an eye open for Sharman as well. He seemed all right to me but perhaps Penny is right."

The twins and Harriet wandered off with Macbeth for a walk over the moor and the others went down to the village and then to the top of the hill together. When Jon and Penny were alone, the latter said, "You're not very happy about all this are you, Jon. I'm wondering whether it might not have been better if Peter and I had stayed in Shropshire. You're not much fun, you know."

"I bet I'm not," Jon said grimly. "If what I suspect about this mine is true and if what I suspect about those two men—Robens and the 'Doctor'—is true, then there could be a lot of trouble. Glad you suggested we do this job together. Haven't seen much of you lately, have I?"

"No," Penny said much too brightly. "No, you haven't, Jon. Makes quite a change, doesn't it?"

At this he laughed but did not say what she was hoping for.

"I'll tell you everything I know about this business after I've been to the Library tomorrow, but I'd like to be sure that none of us will ever see the 'Doctor' or Robens again . . .

Here we are." And he opened the front door of the inn.

A woman came into the hall and greeted them.

"Good evening," Jon said. "We were wondering whether a Mr Warner is staying here. We're anxious to see him."

"I'm sorry, but he left unexpectedly a few hours ago," the woman said, as if she disapproved of her late guest.

"Oh dear," Penny sighed. "What a disappointment! Somebody asked us to look up Mr Warner. I wonder if he happened to mention where he was going?"

"He did not, my dear. He had plenty of luggage and after paying his bill he went off without as much as a 'thank you' for all the trouble he's given the girl in cleaning his room every day. You're the youngsters from Venton's, aren't you? Did you know this Mr Warner?"

"Not well," Jon said quickly. "Not really well, but—"

"Hello, you two," said a familiar voice. "Nice to see you again so soon. Just how well did you know this Mr Warner? I should really like to know that."

With a gasp of surprise Penny turned to see Philip Sharman.

8. *Jon and Penny*

BREAKFAST THE NEXT morning was not very cheerful. Mr Sparrow was testy and went into the shop to deal with his letters as soon as he had finished his meal, and the others agreed with Harriet that he was certainly more worried than they had ever seen him.

"Don't fuss about him too much, Harry," Penny said. "We all like your grandfather and we're going to look after him. I know Jon is going to find out something terrifically important in Whitby this morning. We'll have to start in ten minutes to walk to Goathland to catch the Whitby bus. Why don't some of you come part ot the way with us?"

"Good idea," David agreed, "but somebody should keep an eye on Mr Sharman. When will you be back, Jon?"

"I can find what I'm looking for in half an hour," Jon said. "We'll catch the first bus or train back to Goathland and should be back here for dinner."

"I think somebody should keep an eye on the Wildblood too," Peter said, and then blushed as the door opened quietly and the housekeeper stood on the threshold glaring at them. As soon as the woman realized that Mr Sparrow was not there she spoke in surly fashion and said, "I've my work to do and would be glad if you'd help me clear the table. There's no time to sit around doing nothing in this house after the meal is finished."

Mary smirked at her.

"We *always* help if we can, dear Miss Wildblood. We'll bring everything out to you, so please don't worry."

Miss Wildblood left the room and Peter covered her face with her hands.

"Did she hear? I'm sorry if I gave us away," she whispered.

"I bet she's listening now," Dickie hissed. "I bet she's just behind the door"—and he dashed across the room and flung it open. Miss Wildblood was there and with a cry of triumph Dickie pointed an accusing finger at her.

"Shut up, Dickie," David snapped. "Come and sit down"—and his brother obeyed.

"More and more sinister," Jon said. "You'd all better stop here on guard. We'll be back soon as we can. Good-bye."

"No need for you to come to the Library," Jon said when they got off the bus at Whitby. "See that shrimp stall? I'll meet you there in an hour—that's ten minutes past eleven—and I may be back before then. What are you going to do?"

"I thought I was spending the morning with you, but never mind. I think I'll sit in the sun and maybe walk to the end of the harbour wall. Be as quick as you can, Jon."

Jon gave her a vague sort of salute and crossed the road to ask a policeman the way to the Library. Penny watched him stroll away and wondered, not for the first time, why she allowed him to order her about. Then she smiled to herself and walked along the promenade past the shrimp stall. The sun was warm so she took off her cardigan and leaned on the railing, and watched the river rushing out to the sea. A gull with cruel, curved beak and staring eyes swooped, squawking, just above her head. She ducked instinctively, and as she half turned to face the road she saw a familiar figure slouching along the promenade. Her heart seemed to miss a beat as she recognized the man Robens, who now called himself Warner, and who was causing them so much trouble. She turned her back on him, hoping that she would not be recognized and then, gaining courage, she watched him covertly as he walked away from her towards the mouth of the harbour.

He had looked tired and dispirited. His long, untidy hair was falling over his forehead and, as usual, a smouldering cigarette hung from his lip.

Penny remembered every word the others had told her about this man and recalled his anger at Goathland station and on the walk back through Spaunton. She knew he was an enemy and that he had hurried away from *The Yorkshire Rose* at an hour's notice with a lot of cumbersome luggage. Jon, even now, was trying to prove a case against this man and the "Doctor", and she was suddenly sure of what she must do. She must follow Robens secretly and find out whether he was living in Whitby and what he was doing.

He was not difficult to follow without being seen because he was tall and nobody in Whitby on this spring day looked anything like him. He walked steadily to the end of the promenade without looking back, and then he paused at the end of the road, leaning over the railings for a few moments while Penny dodged behind a parked car. Then he lit a cigarette and turned back towards the town with his hands in his pockets and Penny realized, for the first time, that although this young man was certainly up to no good he was also lonely and unhappy.

She moved from behind the car and crossed the road to the promenade. There were plenty of people about now and as he never turned round he was easy to follow. Soon he crossed the road and turned into a narrow street which climbed up towards the west cliff. Penny hesitated at the corner. The street, but for her fugitive, was empty. If he turned round now he would certainly see her, and although it was possible that he would not recognize her, it was a chance.

Away from the crowds, Penny was not as confident. The houses in this little street were grubby and their windows stared at her like blind eyes. Robens was now fifty yards ahead nearly at the top of the street. She leaned against the wall of the house at the corner, wondering if it would be foolhardy to follow him at once. A skinny cat pushed, purring, against her ankles. When she looked up Robens had disappeared.

Now decision was easy. She forgot the cat and ran up the hill. There was a sharp and unexpected turning to the right into another narrow street and she was just in time to see

Robens turn into a small grocer's shop. She had paused again wondering what to do next, when Robens came out and glanced down the street. In sudden panic Penny turned her back. Surely he would recognize her red head? She listened for hurrying footsteps behind her but there was silence. She turned again and the street was empty!

Without hesitation now she hurried up the street, past the shop and found the narrow entrance to another cobbled street. Only a few seconds had passed since she had turned her back on Robens and now she was once again just in time to see him opening a door half-way up on the left. She shrank back against the wall but he did not look back and stepped into the house and closed the door behind him.

She looked up and saw that this narrow, dead-end street was called Prospect Way. Now surely she had run Robens to earth and could hurry back to Jon with the news that she had found his hiding-place? While she stood hesitating, she noticed that the door through which the man had disappeared was next to another small shop. She might as well be certain about all this and although her heart was thumping with excitement she had, for a moment, lost her fear because she was sure that if Robens suddenly reappeared she could turn and run and that he would never catch her.

She felt proud of herself as she walked steadily up the street trying not to look into the curtained windows of any of the little houses. The little shop was even more unattractive than the grocer's in the next street. She tried to look in, but the window was so grubby that she could not see anything. The door through which Robens had gone was at the other side of the window and Penny guessed correctly that it must be a separate entrance into the house. The shop had no name or number above the window.

It would be easy to bring Jon here and then perhaps together they could go into the shop and make some inquiries about Robens. It did not seem possible that he could actually *live* here, and then with a flash of inspiration she realized that this was exactly the sort of place in which a man who did not want to be recognized might hide. Why wait for Jon? Why not finish the job? She was sure that if Peter had been here alone she would not have hesitated. She would go into the shop and ask some question about Robens, the answer to which would be useful to them. It was ridiculous to be afraid. Robens was not in the shop, and it would only take a moment or two to confirm that he was actually living here, and what Peter could do she wanted to do better.

Penny lifted her chin, opened the shop door and stepped over the threshold. A bell jangled above her head, and as she peered into the gloom a man moved forward out of the shadows, slipped behind her and bolted the shop door. Then a light was switched on and Penny stifled a scream as she realized that the man between her and escape was the "Doctor".

She felt her knees weaken and heard a strange, hoarse voice which must have been her own, whisper, "Don't you dare to touch me," as the man grasped her arm and pulled her under the light.

The shop was small, dark and smelly. Behind the short counter piled with papers, was a slatternly woman in an overall and with a cigarette hanging from her lip. From a room somewhere behind the shop came the sound of the radio playing pop music.

She shook her arm free.

"Take your hands off me and let me go," she raged.

Only the radio broke a long silence. This morning their enemy was wearing a tweed suit and a cap to match. His eyes looked small behind the thick lenses of his spectacles but she could see now that they were cruel eyes. Hard and cold.

"Well! Well!" he said at last. "A little red-headed spitfire. Quite an unexpected meeting, my dear. It was on Goathland station that I had the pleasure of making your acquaintance, I believe. Don't trouble to deny it . . . *What are you doing here?*"

He rapped out the last question with such venom that she stepped back instinctively.

"Where I go is nothing to do with you," she said, struggling to keep her voice steady. "I remember seeing you yesterday, but I'm in Whitby now with my friends and I was exploring and got lost. Please unlock that door and let me go. You know you've no right to keep me here"—and then she turned to the slatternly woman and said, "Tell him to let me go."

Without taking his eyes off Penny, the man spoke to the woman. "You keep quiet. This is nothing to do with you. We're going upstairs and I don't want to be interrupted. If you see any other strange kids snooping about in the street, lock the door again and let me know. Otherwise stay here." Then, to Penny, "Are you coming quietly or have I got to carry you? I'm not going to hurt you if you're sensible and answer a few questions."

Penny considered. It was obvious that she could not escape from the shop now and she shivered at the idea of struggling with him. She looked round at the white-faced woman who would not meet her eyes and knew at once that there would be no help from her.

So she glanced quickly at the "Doctor", twisted her fingers together nervously and looked down as she said:

"I don't know what questions I can answer. All I want to do is to get back to my friends who will be worried and looking for me if I'm not back soon. I can't see why you should bully me. I haven't done anything to you. Please let me go."

"That's much better," the man said as he took her arm again. "That sounds like a sensible young lady talking. Just come upstairs with me, my dear, and we'll have a little chat. I'm sure it won't be long before you are able to join your friends."

She shuddered at his touch as he led her through a curtained doorway at the back of the shop, through a stale-smelling sitting-room in which the radio was still playing and up a dark, narrow stairway. On the landing he pushed past her, opened a door and then dragged her into the room. In a shabby chair by the window Robens was sitting, smoking the inevitable cigarette. The "Doctor" locked the door behind him and pushed Penny gently enough towards a chair as Robens got to his feet.

"Good morning, Robbie," the "Doctor" said coldly. "I'm sure you didn't expect to see me and it's very obvious that you didn't expect to see our charming visitor. Or did you? Do you know who she is?"

Robens sat down again.

"I didn't expect to see either of you and this is one of the interfering children I warned you about. She's one of the gang that put on that act at Goathland yesterday. What's she doing here? And why are you in this stinking hole?"

Penny hoped that they could not hear the beating of her heart. She was wondering whether the "Doctor" in his anger with Robens might forget her. He strode over to the younger man and lashed him in a cold, quiet voice.

"You stupid, blundering fool, Robbie. Why can't you believe me when I tell you how careful you must be? I'm sure that this girl saw you this morning and followed you here. I was in the shop doing some business with the woman and saw you from the window come slouching up the street and go upstairs without even looking round. Then this girl comes along and says she's exploring, but she was close on your heels and for all I know she's followed you for miles. She's got more courage than you've got sense."

Robens got up and faced him.

"I'll not waste my breath on you, nor will I tell you what I think of you in front of her. Anyway, I'm through. I'm off. Do your own work for once. I've had enough. I don't care about the money. I'm through."

The "Doctor" was not impressed.

"You're through here, Robbie. Go and pack your bag, and while you're doing it just remember that you can't be through with me. I know too much about you. By your carelessness you've given yourself away to a pack of children. They followed you yesterday and you've been fooled today. You can't stay here. I'll find you a new home, Robbie, and I'm going to take great care of you in future. While you're packing up I'm going to have a chat with our guest."

Penny looked up in fear as the "Doctor" unlocked the door and Robens, muttering under his breath and not even looking at her, went out of the room. She was frightened because she could see that he was completely in the power of the older man and, in spite of his bluster, had no fight left.

Now she was alone with him. She clenched her hands in her lap and hardly felt the pain of her nails in the soft flesh as he moved his chair into the open doorway so that he was between her and escape, and could also watch the landing. Then he began to talk, but afterwards, when she tried to remember exactly what he said, she was not really sure of all his questions nor of the answers she gave him. He was clever and she was disarmed because he did not try to bully her. He flattered her by treating her as an intelligent adult and did not even ask whether she had been following Robens. He assumed that she had, and there was therefore no opportunity for her to deny it. He asked her how long she had known Mr Sparrow and where she lived and why she was staying at Spaunton. He asked her whether the twins and the other girl—who was Peter—were also staying at Venton's and how many there were in the party. She tried to dodge this question hoping that he did not know about Jon and David, but while she hesitated he said:

"But of course I remember now. Our young friend who, as you know, has been staying in Spaunton, told me that there were two elder boys camping up by the old mine shaft. Who are those boys, my dear, and where do they live?"

Penny remembered Peter's comment about the danger of associating any of them with Shropshire and tried to bluff.

"You mean my cousin? He'll be looking for me everywhere now and I do wish you'd let me go, please. He lives at Rye too in the holidays."

"And the other boy?"

"He's a friend. He lives in London."

"Ah yes. And old Mr Sparrow has a granddaughter who is a member of your happy house-party, I believe, and he's very attached to her?"

She fell into the trap. "Yes, he is. She nearly always stays with him in the holidays. May I go now, please? I promise I'll never come near this place again if you'll let me go."

"I don't suppose you will, my dear . . . Ah! Come along in, Robbie."

The "Doctor" turned again to Penny.

"Now listen carefully because what I have to say is of particular importance. By your interference in matters which are no concern of yours, you and your friends are in danger. You should realize this now if you did not do so before. You all seem to have some regard for Mr Sparrow, so I am going to entrust you with a message for him. Mr Sparrow has had by now the last offer of a very large sum of money for his house, property and land. Will you tell him that unless he accepts it he is not going to like the consequences. You are an intelligent girl and should understand clearly that this is a warning both to all you interfering children and to Mr Sparrow. And don't forget that any nonsense from you—nonsense such as discussing this meeting with the police—could well make things very unpleasant for your old friend Mr Sparrow . . . Do you understand?"

The "Doctor's" warning was spoken quietly and without undue emphasis but Penny shivered as she listened. She knew that he was not bluffing and she was afraid.

"Do you understand me? You and your young friends will be wise to leave Spaunton as soon as possible. Go back to your homes and forget everything."

"How can I go back anywhere if you keep me in this beastly place?" Penny flared.

"No doubt you'll get back to Spaunton eventually, and then you can give old Sparrow his warning. Ready, Robbie? Good."

Robens went out without a backward look. Penny could

see that he was angry, but his fear of his companion was very much greater than anger, and she could now understand why. There was something terrifying about this older, commonplace-looking man. He gave her one last, menacing glance and then followed Robens and locked the door on the outside.

Penny sat still with her hands twisted in her lap. They would expect her to shout or scream for help or bang on the door, so she sat quietly and made no attempt to check a tear that trickled down her nose.

After a little she got up and tried the door, but as she suspected there was no escape there. Her legs felt weak as she walked over to the window and looked down into dingy Prospect Way. She had forgotten all about the time until she looked at her watch and saw that it was five-and-twenty minutes to twelve! She had promised Jon to be at the shrimp stall at ten past eleven at the latest. He would be furious of course, and think that she had forgotten the time and the appointment.

Then she heard voices directly below her, and when she looked down through the window she saw Robens and the "Doctor" walking quickly down Prospect Way. She ran to the door again, shook it and then pummelled it with her clenched fists.

"Let me out!" she shouted. "Unlock the door or I'll smash the window. Let me out! *Let me out!*"

She felt hysteria rising and fought back the tears at the thought of Jon waiting for her on the promenade. She *must* get out.

Again she beat on the door. Nothing happened except that she bruised and grazed her knuckles, and as she stood back and sucked the blood, tears of pain and frustration trickled down her face. Then she sat at the table with her chin in her hands and tried to think. And the more she considered her dilemma the clearer it became that she would never get away from this place unless she used her wits. She tried to imagine what Jon or David would have done and reached the conclusion that it would be best to open the window and when someone came into Prospect Way—and surely someone must come sometime?—she would tell them that she was locked in by mistake and could not make the woman downstairs hear her. That might do for a start.

She looked at her watch and saw that the time was now just after twelve. She went to the door again and tried the handle. It was no longer locked. She pulled it open. The key had gone and must have been removed by the woman in the shop.

She stepped out on to the gloomy landing and remembered that there must be a second staircase leading down directly to the door through which she had seen Robens pass only just over an hour ago. She found it and ran down, but this door was bolted and locked and without a key. There was no escape here so she crept up to the landing again, realizing that she had no alternative but to go down to the room behind the shop.

With wildly-beating heart, Penny stepped slowly down the other staircase leading to the room behind the shop. The door of this room was ajar and she pushed it open gently. There was nobody there although the remains of a meal were on the table. At the far end of the room was another closed door which, she supposed, led to a scullery. On her left was the curtained entrance to the shop. What should she do?

Swiftly she pushed the curtain back, ran for the door, and in seconds was free and running down Prospect Way as if the devil was after her. She ran until her mouth was dry and a stitch stabbed at her side. The air was fresh and clean and the sun was shining. The gulls sailed over the roof-tops and when she reached the promenade she stopped for breath. It seemed impossible that Prospect Way was only a few hundred yards away and that there she had been locked in, questioned and threatened.

She crossed the road and ran to the shrimp stall. Jon was not there. She ran on to the fish market but he was not there either. She turned back towards the shrimp stall and played with herself an old, childish game. She closed her eyes while counting five, saying to herself. "When I open them again he'll be there waiting for me."

But he was not. She ran back into the town and asked the way to the Public Library. She asked for Jon there, and they remembered him leaving over an hour ago. She ran out into the crowded street again in a panic. Where had he gone? Perhaps he was at the shrimp stall now? Why could he not have been patient and waited at the place where they had arranged to meet? Perhaps he was so angry that he had gone back to Spaunton or Goathland by bus?

She ran to the bus station and learned that the last bus to Goathland had left two hours ago.

What should she do now? Telephone Venton's? But Jon could not have got back there and surely he would not desert her? Of course he would not. He must still be looking for her in Whitby. Perhaps he was at the shrimp stall now?

She ran back towards the quay, but when she came to the swing bridge crossing the Esk which all north-south traffic had to cross, a policeman in the middle of the road was holding up pedestrians. As she stood waiting on the kerb to cross, the constable deliberately smiled at her. He looked nice and she gave him a watery sort of smile in return. He held up the traffic and as the people began to cross the road he beckoned to her. Perhaps she should tell him about Prospect Way, but would he believe her and wasn't it more important to find Jon? But why should he want her specially?

The policeman smiled at her again.

"Lost your boy-friend, miss? Chap with untidy hair and specs. He's looking for a red-head."

Penny could have kissed him but she could only nod.

"He asked me to look out for you. Said you were scatter-brained. He thought you might be sightseeing but he seemed in a bit of a state. He's gone up to the church to see if you were there and had forgotten the time, and if you weren't there he's going to look round the ruins of the abbey."

She gave him a radiant smile and he winked at her as he

held up the traffic again for her to cross. She raced over the bridge, turned to the left along a narrow street of old houses and then, at the end, saw the long, long flight of worn, stone steps winding up towards the church on the edge of the cliff. There were plenty of people using the steps but she was nearly at the top when she saw Jon coming down. Her heart seemed to jump into her throat and then banged away so furiously that she stopped and leaned against the iron hand-rail, waiting for him to come to her.

"You little idiot! Why weren't you at the shrimp stall? Why can't you keep an appointment like anybody else? I suppose you know I've been searching the town for you for hours. I found what I wanted in the Library after twenty minutes, but now I can't even trust you to be in the place where we arranged to meet. I suppose you've been having a look at the shops?"

She turned and looked at him. His face was white with anger.

Her temper flared. "How dare you speak to me as if I was one of the twins? You only think of yourself, don't you? You great stuck-up, conceited lout. And you think I'd deliberately keep you waiting and you don't even ask what has happened to me. You don't care. *You* don't care whether I've been k-k-kidnapped and locked up in a beastly, smelly shop by the 'Doctor' and Robens . . . *You don't care* . . ."

His strong hands gripped her shoulders and swung her round to face him. She struggled for a moment and then looked up at him, and in a flash she knew that he was not really angry but frightened because he had lost her, and with that realization she burst into tears and clung to the lapels of his jacket. She just didn't care. She snivelled against the rough tweed and even when he passed her his own handkerchief she held on to him with one hand.

After a while she stepped back, wiped her eyes and said in a small and rather choky voice, "Sorry, Jon. I've made idiots of both of us."

"Oh no, you haven't. I've been a fool for a very long time, but don't scare me like this again."

Then he took her firmly by the hand with the bruised, grazed knuckles, but she hardly noticed the pain—led her up the steps and then across the churchyard to one of the seats on the edge of the cliff.

"Now tell me everything," he said.

She told him. What had happened only an hour or so ago did not seem important now, but it was still vivid and she wasted no words. He hardly interrupted, but when she admitted her panic when she banged on the locked door, he loosened the grip of his fingers and looked at her hand. When he saw the bruises and the blood he did something he had never done before. Without any shyness he lifted her hand and kissed it gently.

"Go on, Penny. Tell me everything. How did you get out?"

When she had finished he released her hand and stood up.

"We've got to hurry, Penny," he said. "There's a lot to do and after this morning's effort we must all try and stick together. We're really on to something now and we mustn't separate again. I found what I wanted in the paper. I knew I'd read something a few weeks ago about the government being willing to help any private owners of land to search for uranium. I'm sure now of what I suspected. Robens has found deposits of uranium in Venton's old mine and that's why the 'Doctor' is trying to buy out Mr Sparrow who now owns it . . . Come on . . . Are you all right now?"

She stood up and smiled at him.

"Yes I am, Jon. I don't care what happens now. I'm feeling fine. It's most peculiar, as Dickie would say, but I'm feeling happy, too."

9. The Second Threat

SOON AFTER JON AND PENNY had gone to Whitby, the twins and Harriet went up on the moor with Macbeth. Peter and David went with them as far as the caravan and then turned back.

"This isn't much of a holiday really, David," Peter said. "We're not having fun, are we? I'm beginning to wish we were all in Shropshire. I wouldn't have minded going into Whitby either. Why don't we go off on our own for the day, like Jon and Penny?"

"I don't see why we shouldn't tomorrow," David agreed. "Jon is after something important, though, and I think we should wait until they come back and hear his news. I'm wondering if we've gone as far as we can on this business? Mr Sparrow was very touchy at breakfast. One of his letters upset him. He's really worried about all this, Peter, and I've even been wondering whether we all ought to go home because we may be in his way. Anyway, there's no reason why we shouldn't go for a walk now, but we'd better tell the old man we're all out for the morning. I'd like to know more about Philip Sharman too. He's a mystery."

"Too many mysteries," Peter sighed.

Mr Sparrow looked very sad when they found him in the shop. He was sitting at his desk and as they came in he folded a letter and put it in his pocket.

"Well, my dears. I was just thinking of you all. I have something important to tell you. Where are the others?"

David explained that Jon and Penny were in Whitby and that the twins and Harriet were up on the moor.

"We were just talking about you too, sir," he went on. "We know that you're very worried about these men trying to buy Venton's and we want to help you if we can. If we're in the way here, though, do please say so."

"We don't want to go," Peter added as she touched the old man's hand affectionately. "We love being here, but if we do go back to Shropshire we'll take Harriet with us if you like. Would everything be easier for you if we weren't here?"

The old man put an arm round her shoulders.

"No, my dear. It would not be easier for me, but thank you for offering to go. I was going to tell you all of a sudden decision I have made. You can explain to the others later and give Harriet my love. In half an hour I am leaving for London. I do not expect to be away for more than two days and I must therefore close the shop. I have told you that I am under considerable pressure to sell my property here and the offer which came this morning is very tempting. I do not want to sell, but because I am sure that somebody has discovered something of value here, I want to discuss the matter fully with Mr Venton. Although this place is virtually mine I am sure Mr Venton should know what is happening. I personally will not be bullied or bribed into selling just because somebody else wants this property. I would like you all to continue your holiday and I will arrange for Miss Wildblood to look after you. I have, in fact, already asked her to do so and she has agreed."

"But Grandpa Sparrow, we don't trust Miss Wildblood. We think she's been spying on you and we know she was in touch with that detestable man Warner," Peter said.

"Nonsense, my dear. Miss Wildblood is certainly eccentric but she is harmless. You mustn't read more into this situation than actually exists. I trust you older ones to look after the others—indeed you are responsible for them until I return. Although the shop must be closed, I would like to think that you are not all out all the time."

"Of course," David said. "By the time you're back again we may have found out some more. We shall guard the mine as well as the house."

"Thank you, my boy. Here is a spare key, and here, on this slip of paper my telephone number in London . . . Now

I must go and pack because the taxi will be here in ten minutes. I shall lock the shop now."

"I don't like this much, David," Peter said as the old man went upstairs. "He's very worried."

David nodded. "I wish Jon and Penny would come back. I really couldn't say more to him, could I? If Jon has found anything really important we could telephone London to-night, I suppose. Better not say any more to Mr Sparrow now. He's made up his mind to go and nothing much can happen here in twenty-four hours or so."

But David was wrong.

Ten minutes later they said "Good-bye" to Mr Sparrow and as they went back into the house to see Miss Wildblood, the telephone rang.

"I'll answer it," David said with a meaning look at Peter. "Will you fix up everything with Miss Wildblood."

He did not recognize the pleasant voice at first.

"May I speak to Mr Sparrow, please . . . Not there at the moment? I see. This is Philip Sharman. I think you must be David Morton. Good. Listen, David. I met your twins and Harriet Sparrow on the moor and they're coming back to lunch with me at the pub, if nobody minds. We were talking about the Roman road and I'd like to take you up to see it. Will you four come down here presently and we could go together this afternoon?"

David was suddenly suspicious. No sooner had they got rid of Robens than Sharman appeared, and it looked now as if he was going to be difficult to shake off. He wondered too whether the twins and Harriet really were there.

"You still there, David? What about it?"

"The others are out now, Mr Sharman. Thanks for suggesting the Roman road but I must see what Jon and Penny would like to do. May I speak to Harriet, please?" This was the test. Was Harriet really there? She was, for Sharman merely told him to hold on and, in a few moments, David was nearly deafened by her excited "Hello, David! It's Harriet. Grandpa won't mind us staying down here to lunch with Mr Sharman, will he? We're having a lot of fun and he wants to take us up to this mysterious Roman road presently. Will you all come?"

"Now listen, Harry, and don't fuss. Your grandfather has had to go to London suddenly to see Mr Venton, but he'll probably be back tomorrow night. He sent his love. Don't tell the twins or Mr Sharman about Mr Sparrow, and I think you'd all better come back here after lunch as Jon and Penny aren't back from Whitby yet and we'd better talk things over. Tell Mr Sharman that maybe some of us could go to the Roman road tomorrow. Don't worry about your grandfather and don't answer too many questions about him. See you later . . . 'Bye."

He heard her gasp of surprise just before he rang off but he did not want to give her time to argue.

Peter ran to meet him as he closed the shop door.

"You wanted me to keep the Wildblood away, didn't you, David? She's gone now and I've told her that we'll call her over if we want her. I think she's sinister but I'm not sure yet whether she's as simple as she seems to be. Who was that?"

He told her.

"I can't make up my mind about Sharman either, Peter. Why should he suddenly want to make a fuss of the others and ask them out to lunch? Do you think I ought to have told them to come back here now?"

"I don't think it matters if they don't tell him too much. Mr Sharman is a wheedler, though. He might get something out of Harry but it's too late now to do anything about it. I'd rather talk to Jon and Penny before they come back anyway. I wish they'd come. It's after twelve."

While they were waiting they wrote letters home, but at ten minutes past one, when the shepherd's pie was beginning to dry up, they started their meal. They had second helpings, but still there was no sign of the Warrenders.

"I suppose they're just amusing themselves and have decided to eat in Whitby," David grumbled. "The least they could do is to telephone. They're selfish."

"No more than we are," Peter said. "We should telephone if we could and so would they. I'm worried about them. This is a beastly day—everything has gone wrong and we're all separated and I don't like it. Let's walk to Goathland and meet them. Come on, David. The shop is closed and we'll lock the side door and take the key."

As it happened they had only just reached the top of the hill and turned into the road to Goathland, when a car passed them at speed and pulled up about a hundred yards beyond them. Peter turned round to see what had happened as the driver sounded his horn. Then Jon and Penny got out and waved "Good-bye" as the car drove down into Spaunton.

"They must have got a lift," David said. "I bet they've had their lunch and I bet they don't say they're sorry."

He would have lost both bets.

Penny ran to meet him. She looked excited and bright-eyed but pale. Jon looked grim.

"Were you coming to meet us?" he said. "Sorry we're late but we misssed the bus and were lucky to get a lift. We're hungry too because we haven't had anything to eat. We've had quite a morning one way and another. Penny had been kidnapped by the 'Doctor' and Robens, and I'm now convinced that there are uranium deposits in Spaunton mine. And Penny has got a warning for old man Sparrow and we've got to tell him about all this at once."

"You can't," David said. "He's gone to London, and the other kids are being entertained by Sharman at *The Yorkshire Rose*. Tell us the worst as we walk back and finish your story while you're eating, but don't say too much to the twins and Harriet yet. We couldn't tell Harry over the telephone how worried we are about her grandfather."

Jon and Penny's stories were not finished until they had finished the shepherd's pie and then before the others could comment, the telephone bell rang.

"I'll go," David said. "Tell them our story, Pete."

He shut the door between the shop and sitting-room and sat behind Mr Sparrow's desk as he lifted the receiver and announced his number. He did not recognize the voice that replied.

"May I speak to Mr Sparrow, please? The matter is personal and very urgent."

"Mr Sparrow is not here. Who is it speaking, please? I can take a message or perhaps he will ring you when he comes back."

"When he comes back, you say? Will he be long? I was thinking of coming in the car to see him this afternoon or evening. Who is it speaking?"

"I'm a friend of Mr Sparrow's and I'm staying here. Who shall I say is calling him now? It's no use coming here to see him because the shop is closed until he returns."

"But when will that be? I must get into touch with him at once. Do you mean that he is not in Spaunton?"

"No, he isn't. You give me your name and telephone number and I'll ask him to telephone you when he comes back tomorrow."

"I see. Not till tomorrow. Will you kindly give me the number of where he is staying now. I must speak to him. I do assure you that it will be to Mr Sparrow's benefit."

David was suspicious.

"I'm sorry but I can't do that. If he rings me tonight I'll give him your message."

"Very well," the voice said, still smoothly and calmly. "Listen carefully. Tell Mr Sparrow to return to Spaunton immediately and to accept the offer he received this morning. This sounds dramatic, but unless he does so within twenty-four hours, what he cares for most in the world is likely to get damaged or mislaid. Get that message to him."

There was a click and the line went dead. David replaced the receiver and was still staring ahead when Harriet opened the door and ran into the shop.

"David!" she whispered. "Whatever has happened? You look as if you've seen a ghost."

10. *The "Doctor" at Home*

THE TIME IS the early afternoon of the following day and the scene is a deserted stone quarry cut into the side of a little hill.

About two hundred yards away is a row of four ugly, red-brick cottages built at the beginning of the century to house the men who worked in the quarry. Two of these cottages are in a state of decay, and a third seems to be untenanted but is in much better condition.

But it is the fourth cottage nearest to the derelict quarry which is most interesting because there are curtains across the windows, a wisp of smoke coming from the chimney and, most remarkable of all, telephone wires running from it.

Another odd thing about these lonely cottages is that there is no road leading to them. A faint track can be seen behind them running under the telephone wire, and there are signs of another path from the door of the occupied cottage. This is interesting because it leads from what was once a tiny front garden, through the tangle of weeds to a single railway line running parallel to the fronts of the cottages. This line runs, on a slight down gradient, away to the right and then curves out of sight round the shoulder of the far end of the hill over which the telephone wires are carried. To the left it runs obviously uphill for two hundred yards before vanishing into the gloomy mouth of a tunnel burrowed under the hill. Although weeds now grow between the sleepers and at the side of the track, a careful observer would notice that the rails, although not bright, are certainly not as rusty between the tunnel and the cottages as might be expected. He would notice too that the points had been oiled recently, and that a strong pull on the lever at the side of the track would slide them into place so that a goods wagon, a railway carriage or even a locomotive, after emerging from the tunnel, would leave the main track, rattle over the points and run into the deserted quarry.

At about ten minutes to three the door of the occupied cottage opened and a woman stepped out on to the weed-covered path. She was bareheaded with untidy, black hair, and she stood for a moment by the little gate which had once opened into the garden. After a little, she walked through the rough grass towards the railway line, and when she reached the track she turned towards the tunnel with her head tilted, as if she was listening.

There seemed nothing to hear but bird song and the whisper of a little breeze rustling the long grass. Suddenly the woman looked more alert, and after a quick glance at the tunnel she turned and ran clumsily back to the cottage, went in and closed the door.

Then there was a roar and a rattle and out from the mouth of the tunnel rushed one of those flat, four-wheeled trolleys which are propelled by a lever that can be worked backwards and forwards. The man on the trolley was the "Doctor". As his unusual vehicle approached the points, he applied a brake so that it passed over them, slowed down and stopped opposite the cottages.

The "Doctor" stepped off and stood for a moment at the edge of the long grass and looked around. Then he glanced at the telephone wires rising up over the hill, looked at the watch on his wrist and walked briskly up to the garden gate and pushed open the door of the cottage.

The "Doctor" had come home.

The door opened into a narrow hall with a door on the left. The woman was waiting to welcome him.

"Good afternoon, sir. Very pleasant weather. You'll let me know when you would like your tea, sir?"

"Good afternoon, Edith. I will most certainly let you

know when I want something. Anything to report? Has the telephone rung?"

"No, sir. I haven't heard it, sir."

"You have not left the house, Edith?"

"Oh no, sir! As if I would, sir!"

"I'm sure you would if you thought I should never find out. *You will remember to do as you are told, Edith.* Now run along to your kitchen and stay there until I call you."

She shrank back against the wall as the "Doctor" opened the door of the front room which, although not expensively furnished, was comfortable. There was a carpet on the floor, an easy chair by the old-fashioned grate in which a fire was laid, and a table with an oil-lamp. In the far corner was a desk of the sort sometimes seen in second-hand furniture shops—a desk with a roll top which could be locked down over the contents. On the top of the desk was a telephone receiver and on a small table by the fireplace, a transistor radio.

The "Doctor" put on his glasses and consulted his watch again.

"Due in three minutes," he muttered. "Today I should be able to clinch this business. A real scare would make this stubborn old man see sense. Once that is through, I shall have to do something about Robens who is becoming unreliable."

Then the telephone rang and with a self-satisfied smile the "Doctor" lifted the instrument from the desk and took it, on its long cord, to the easy chair. He sat down, lifted the receiver and said quietly:

"Who is that? Ah yes! Of course you are punctual. Just hold on for a moment or two if you please."

He put down the telephone, and on tiptoe crossed quickly to the door which he suddenly flung open. There was nobody in the hall, and as the kitchen door was closed he went back into his room and picked up the receiver again. But this was one of the few occasions when he was not clever enough. The woman Edith had been caught like this before, and it was not until the sitting-room door had closed for the second time that she came out of the kitchen, crept down the hall in her stockinged feet and put her ear to the thin panel of the door.

Although he was speaking quietly, she could hear everything he said. He sounded very sure of himself.

"Now then, Robbie. Not so excited, if you please. Just tell me one thing at a time and I will ask the questions. What is the news of the old man? What do you say? Not back until this evening? The six o'clock at Pickering. Sure? She really has checked up? Yes. I suppose we can trust her and now we have to move quickly. Listen carefully, Robbie, because there are to be no mistakes. *She's got to be taken now* . . . Yes, I mean within the next hour or two. I don't care where the others are or what they are doing but you and Amy have got to make it work. Get her away from the others. Get her in the car . . . *How*, you fool? . . . I've talked to Amy about this. The kid will trust her—or she'll listen to her anyway, and that was the idea, wasn't it? . . . Bring her to the old barn and wait with her there until Edith comes for her. If Edith is *not* there when you arrive, run the car in, lock the door and wait for her . . . Not until we've got the child must you leave and then you can take Amy back with you . . . *What about the old boy?* . . . Don't worry about that. I'll look after him . . . What's on your mind now? What did you say? *What about the other kids?* . . . What about them? Not scared of them, are you? Clever lot and a bit suspicious? You're crazy, Robbie, and you're going soft. Just get on with the job and don't argue . . . What about the other chap? Still hanging about and friendly with them, is he? . . . All right, Robbie. I'll look after him presently, but meanwhile try not to let yourself be seen. You're supposed to have left the place, but we must get this fellow away from Spaunton . . . Got everything clear, Robbie? If you haven't managed the job by five, telephone me here again, but you must stay in the barn with her until someone comes . . . That will do. Don't fail but there's no need to be rough with her . . ."

Edith scuttered back to the kitchen while her master replaced the telephone on the top of the desk.

"Edith," he shouted. "Bring me some tea and toast and be sharp about it because I've got a nice little job for you."

11. *Where's Harriet?*

BREAKFAST AT VENTON'S next morning was a noisy meal and Harriet seemed in much better spirits. When at last they were sitting down together with their eggs and bacon and the kitchen door was closed, she said, "Now please do be quiet and let me say something. Last night when we spoke to Grandpa on the telephone was so exciting that I've nearly forgotten what's going to happen today, except he's coming back here with Mr Venton tonight. Did he sound worried, David, when you gave him that awful message? When I spoke to him he just told us not to worry and that he would see us all soon after six. He said they would get a taxi from Pickering, didn't he?"

Harriet had a clear and carrying voice, and as she spoke in the sudden silence for which she had asked, David frowned.

"Not so loud, Harry. If the Wildblood really is a spy she would be able to hear every word you say in the kitchen. She asked me just now when Mr Sparrow was coming back and I said I wasn't sure. We must speak quietly and it would be better if we didn't talk about it until after breakfast."

"This is ridiculous," Peter said indignantly. "Why should we whisper? We're guests in this house and even if that woman has heard that Mr Sparrow is coming back this evening what does it matter? I suggest we all go out together today and enjoy ourselves and try and forget these nasty people. Nobody can hurt Mr Sparrow if he isn't here, and we can lock up the house and shop."

"Wildblood has a key," Jon said quietly as he passed Penny the toast. "She can get in and we can't stop her."

Dickie spoke out of the side of his mouth. "Listen to me,

brother. There's one way to deal with that old telephone. Cut it. Cut the wire," and then, with a meaning look at the closed door he emptied the sugar into his pocket, grabbed the bowl, tiptoed to the kitchen door and flung it open. Miss Wildblook was sitting at the table eating her breakfast and the look she gave him was unfriendly.

"Hello, Miss Wildblood," Dickie said cheekily. "Sorry to disturb you but acksherley we've run out of sugar. Please could we have some more? We're quite fabulous about sugar in our family."

"Greedy, I'd call it," she grumbled as she went to the cupboard. "I'll swear I filled that bowl this morning. Here you are."

Dickie retired with profuse thanks and closed the door firmly behind him.

"There you are," he said, again out of the side of his mouth. "What did I tell you? She wasn't acksherley listening at the door but she might have been. She was once before . . . An' it's no use you looking at me all sneering like that, David. Mary an' me think you're much too solemn and serious and grown up about this adventure. You're getting tiresome if you know what we mean."

David was about to reply when Mary forestalled him. "So you are, David. So is everybody except us twins an' Harriet—and after all it's *her* grandfather that all the fuss is about—an' perhaps Petah . . . We like Mr Sharman and he likes us and he wants to take us to the Roman road today as we couldn't go yesterday afternoon. Let's do that an' take a picnic."

"What do you think, Jon?" David asked.

"Not a bad idea, but we mustn't forget the warning for Mr Sparrow you took on the telephone yesterday. 'Something that he valued very much might become damaged or mislaid,' wasn't it?"

David nodded. "That's it, but Mr Sparrow didn't seem particularly upset when I told him. He just laughed and said, 'Nonsense, boy! Don't worry. We'll settle everything tomorrow night.' He sounded cheerful, didn't he, Harry?',

"Oh yes. He sounded wonderful when he spoke to me Happy, like he used to be in London and when he first came here. He told me that we were all to enjoy ourselves. He's coming on the train that gets to Pickering at six o'clock."

Almost before she had finished speaking the door opened and Miss Wildblood came in with a smirk on her face and another bowl of sugar in her hand.

"Thought you might be running short of sugar," she said as she banged the bowl down in front of Dickie. "Perhaps I could now be told how many will be in for *another* meal midday."

They looked at her in respectful silence and then all burst out laughing. Then Penny, who seemed to have a soft spot for the Wildblood, got up and put a hand on her arm.

"Please don't mind us. We weren't laughing at you—only at one of our silly private jokes. We'd all like a packed lunch, please, and Peter and I will be out in a minute to help you cut sandwiches. And don't worry about the table now. We'll clear away when we've finished."

The woman stared at her and then went back to the kitchen.

"She had us that time," David admitted. "She knows now when Mr Sparrow will be back and I suppose we're now committed to go out for the day, but do we have to go with Mr Sharman?"

"You're too suspicious, David," Peter said. "Mr Sparrow trusts him and he's offered to show us these places so let's go with him. If he's with us we can keep an eye on him and he can't get back here and poke round, can he?"

"Let's go then," Jon agreed. "But I'm still worried by the telephone threat."

"I know what's going to happen," Dickie said. "Somebody is going to creep in here and fill the cellar with whatever they blow things up with, and blow the whole place up like Guy Fawkes. I hope they do it today while we're out and before Grandpa Sparrow comes back . . . Mary an' me will now just run down the hill to *The Yorkshire Rose* and tell Mr Sharman we'll all be ready in an hour."

The others let them go but Harriet was not too pleased because she had to make their beds. There were no further difficulties with Miss Wildblood who was reasonably good-humoured about the sandwiches and twenty minutes later they were being greeted by the twins and Macbeth at *The Yorkshire Rose*.

"Hope you've got plenty of food," Dickie said. "It's hungry sort of weather. Mr Sharman—he says we can all call him Philip—is inside getting *his* sandwiches."

"So we're to call him Philip, are we?" David said. "I don't think I like that idea very much. We must all remember not to tell him too much about our affairs and particularly Mr Sparrow's business . . . 'Morning, Mr Sharman. Thanks for putting up with us today."

"None of you mind a good walk, do you?" Sharman said. "It's nearly three miles from here to the beginning of the Roman road and another two on to Coram Street across the moors. I know the way and it's rough going."

It was difficult to be suspicious of Philip Sharman this morning, and before long even David was asking him questions about the deserted village and listening to his answers with interest.

He led them up on to the moor on the side of Spaunton which they had not yet explored. When they were up, high above the village, he passed David his binoculars.

"Look through those and you can easily see the new cover Mr Sparrow has put on the mine shaft. From just about here, with these glasses, you could watch anybody who was snooping about. Anybody there now?"

The last question was asked so naturally and casually that, for a moment, David hardly realized its significance. He altered the focus of the glasses and with a sudden shock realized that he could see the girls' caravan, their tents *and* the mine shaft.

"Anybody there, David? You've left Venton's empty today, I suppose? Maybe it doesn't matter."

David handed back the glasses and looked at the others

to see whether they had noticed what Sharman was saying. Jon and Penny very obviously had done so.

"Thanks," David said. "They're fine glasses and I can see our camp. There's nobody there. Why should there be?"

Sharman did not answer this question but began to tell them more about the Roman road.

"It starts and finishes suddenly and was only discovered about seventy years ago. When we get there you will see how it runs along the ridge of Wheeldale Moor and although, after about a mile, the actual paving stones disappear we know that the ancient road goes straight on to Stape and Cawthorn. This was one of the roads up which the Roman legions marched on their way to the north-east coast. Do you like the idea of walking where the Roman soldiers marched, Harriet?"

"Yes, I do. My grandfather has taught me to like old things. I wish we could see the legions marching in their helmets and armour and carrying their golden eagles flashing in the sun."

So they walked over the moor and found a rough, grassy track that led them down into a valley with a rushing beck at the bottom. They met nobody until Mr Sharman showed them a bungalow where lived a woman who is the custodian of the road because it is now cared for by the government. Here they all signed a visitors' book and got tickets which permitted them to walk the way the Romans trod. Then they climbed up again through two rough pastures until they saw ahead of them a gate in a stone wall.

"The road starts at the other side of that gate," Sharman said, as the twins and Harriet with Macbeth raced ahead.

They all rested at the gate and looked at the rough, weather-worn stones of the road which stretched away up the moor like a grubby white ribbon on a brown carpet.

"But these aren't the *actual* stones, are they?" Harriet asked. "Surely the Romans didn't really walk on these, because they're not level and they're too rough. We couldn't walk on them, so how could they with all their armour and their chariots and things—if they had chariots?"

Philip Sharman puffed at his pipe.

"It's more or less in its original state, Harriet. Most of the stones must be part of the old paving although I agree that the road would have to be more level for the legions to march along it."

"Let's march then!" Dickie shouted. "Let's try it"—and he stepped on to the road. Mary and Harriet followed him, and just as Penny said, "Who'd be a Roman soldier? I'm going to stick to this nice, smooth green path at the side," Harriet slipped on one of the stones and fell heavily.

For a moment she lay still while the twins, each poised on a big stone, looked back at her. Then Jon jumped on to the road and picked her up in his arms.

She was half laughing and half crying when he set her down on a big rock at the edge of the grass verge and the others crowded round.

"I'm sorry to be such a fool," she said as she blinked her tears away. "It's my ankle. It's swelling! It hurts."

Peter and Sharman went down on their knees and examined her foot. They made her move it and she tried fairly successfully to stand on it.

"Bad luck," Sharman said. "You've sprained it, Harriet, but I'm sure you haven't broken anything. One of you run along until you find water and soak my handkerchief."

Dickie dashed along the side of the road and was back in a few minutes. Harriet squealed when the cold compress was bound tightly round her ankle but admitted, when she tried to walk, that it still hurt.

"I've spoiled it all for you," she whispered tragically. "I'm sure it will be better soon but I suppose that I shall have to go back to Spaunton. You must go on without me."

They looked at one another uneasily. Then Mary said, "Of course we can't leave Harry alone anywhere. This is just a horrid thing that has happened to her. I nearly slipped myself. We can see this deserted village place another day."

Dickie looked shocked at this suggestion but Harriet, after giving Mary a grateful smile protested that it was silly for all the others to give up their expedition just for her, and that if she could be helped down to the road by the bungalow she could either stay there or get a lift. This seemed to be a reasonable idea and as Mary now refused to leave Harriet, Peter offered to go with them.

"We can't let Mary be responsible for Harriet," she said to David. "I'll go with them. I don't really mind."

After some more argument this was agreed, but David insisted on walking back to the road with them so that he could carry Harriet on his back some of the way if necessary and make sure that they got a lift.

"Wait for me half an hour at the end of the road," he said to Sharman. "If I don't come then, you'd better go on and I'll try and follow you. I've got a map and know the direction."

So the party split up and Harriet, holding on to David and Peter, limped downhill to the bungalow. Then David carried her up to the road and there they sat in the sun, hoping for a lift. They waited only five minutes when a butcher's van came along and stopped when they waved.

After that it was easy. The driver was able to take them to Spaunton and so it was only a short while later that Peter and Mary helped Harriet out of the car outside Venton's in time to see Miss Wildblood coming out of the telephone box. They remembered afterwards that they had never seen her look so wild and excited. She was astonished to see them but seemed genuinely interested and concerned about Harriet.

"I'd better be coming in with you and making you a cup of tea and helping you with that ankle. I wasn't expecting any of you for hours yet. Where are the others?"

"Thank you, Miss Wildblood, but you needn't bother," Peter said quickly. "We can manage. Harriet has only sprained her ankle and it's better already. Isn't it, Harry?"

Harriet agreed, but still limped when she tried to put weight on the foot so, as the housekeeper insisted on coming in, there was nothing they could do to stop her. They noticed that she used her own key to open the side door.

"Now you'd better lie down on the sofa in the sitting-room and we'll bind that ankle up again," she said. "Come along now, you girls. Go easy as you help her. Where did you say you done it, dearie?"

Harriet explained about the stones on the Roman road.

"Aye. I've heard tell o' that place," she admitted. "I've never seen it though. And the boys and the dog? How long will they be? And the young chap from the pub going with 'em seems a bit odd, don't it. What would you say he was up to, miss?"

The last question she put quite sharply to Peter who was nearly taken off her guard. The Wildblood was certainly acting in a very peculiar way, and they had never heard her so talkative. It was rather odd and Peter decided not to answer any of her questions.

"If you would make us a cup of tea and cut some bread and butter, that would be a great help," she suggested. "Mary and I can put a fresh compress on Harriet's ankle."

Miss Wildblood nodded and then went through into the shop and peered out into the street.

"Looks like a storm," she muttered when she came back. "I'll put the kettle on but I'll be glad if you'll watch it while I'm over at the cottage. I'll be back soon."

"I'm a fraud really," Harriet said as Peter began to bind on the new cold compress. "It really is better already and I'm so very sorry that I've spoiled your day for you."

"You're not the fraud," Mary said suddenly. "That old witch is the fraud. What's she doing now? First of all she wants to help, then she goes away just when she could do something. She's excited and most perkewler and I wish my twin was here. Watch the kettle, Petah. I'm going to see what she's doing."

She was away barely five minutes and when she returned Peter was in the kitchen cutting bread and butter and carrying on a shouted conversation with Harriet in the next room. As Mary closed the back door, Peter glanced up and saw that she was looking very serious. There was a great bond between these two. Indeed Peter was an almost ideal elder sister to Mary.

Now the little girl stood with her back to the door and said quietly, "She went straight into that telephone box again. She didn't go into her cottage. There's something funny going on, Petah. Why didn't she telephone from here if it's urgent? Why does she want to go and telephone again just as soon as we come back? I'll tell you why—"

Peter put down the bread knife.

"You mean she's telling somebody that we've arrived just when they expected the house to be empty?"

"That's what I mean, Petah. I wish the others were here. I don't like what's happening."

Peter didn't like it either but didn't want to alarm the two younger girls by showing them that she was uneasy.

Then Harriet, from the other room, accused them of whispering, so Mary went in and told her what had happened and Peter heard them giggling together while she made the tea. She was just putting some plates on a tray when the housekeeper came back looking more excited than before.

"Now you go in the other room, miss, and I'll bring this in to you . . . Run along . . . I'm supposed to be looking after you while Mr Sparrow is away and that's what I'm going to do . . . I just had to go over the road for a minute, but here I am now, so you go and see whether that child's ankle is better. It's got to be rested. She must stay where she is and rest it, but if you and the twin want to go out and meet your friends I'll stay with the child."

"I've never heard her talk so much," Harriet whispered to Peter as she sat down beside her. "All the same I'm hungry and maybe that's why I've got a headache. The swelling is going down, Peter. Perhaps presently we could go for a walk and try it?"

"You must rest it, miss. That's what you must do." Miss Wildblood said as she came in with the tray. "You mustn't go out. Now get on with your tea. You must all be hungry."

They looked at each other in surprise but had little or no chance to discuss her while they were eating because she kept coming through the room and going into the shop to look out of the window. Twice Peter suggested that she might just as well go home as they could now manage, and eventually she said, "Very well, miss, but there's something I ought to tell Mr Sparrow, but as he's not here and you don't know when the others will be back I reckon I'd better tell you. There's some odd goings-on round here and I don't like it. There's been some strangers hanging about round your caravan up on the hill for an hour or more. It's just on four o'clock now and I see them first just before you come back. It's not for *me* to say, o' course, but if I were you I'd take Mary up for company and see what they're up to. Strangers they were. A man and woman so far as I could see. I didn't really want to worry you, miss, but it's your caravan. Maybe you lock it? Maybe you don't, but I'd run up there and see what's going on. I'll stay with Harriet until you come back and just wash up these things."

Peter was puzzled. The woman was obviously in earnest and very excited, and no doubt her concern about the strangers on the hill accounted for her peculiar behaviour since their return. Peter could not remember now whether she had locked the caravan.

"We'll all go," Harriet said suddenly. "It won't hurt me to try the ankle now and we can walk slowly."

Peter was not so sure. The way up the moor was rough and there seemed no sense in Harriet risking it. Miss Wildblood was more definite.

"Of course I'm nobody here, but Mr Sparrow told me I was to look after you all and it would be just plain silly to risk this child's ankle by walking about on it now. I'm saying she should stay here and rest that foot and I'll stay with her."

"Miss Wildblood is right, Peter," Mary said. "I'll stay with Harriet too, while you run up to the caravan."

But this suggestion did not please Miss Wildblood.

"No, no!" she cried excitedly. "You two girls go up together. Two's better than one. I'll stay with Harriet but you should go at once. Both of you."

"I'm *not* going with Peter. I'm going to stay with Harriet," Mary said firmly. "Please hurry, Peter. Just go and look and come back quickly."

"Very well," Peter agreed. "I expect the strangers Miss Wildblood saw are only hikers but they're trespassing and I'll go and tell them so. Perhaps I shall meet them on their way down to the village. I won't be long."

Outside, everything was quiet and still, and as she hurried up the steep path to the moor a flash of lightning split the sullen sky and far, far away the thunder muttered a warning of the gathering storm.

She paused for breath when she came in sight of the caravan. She could not see anybody there so went on more slowly and much relieved. The caravan door was locked, and although the windows were open there were no signs that anybody had been there or had tried to break in. Having gone so far, she thought she might as well look at the boys' camp up by the mine shaft two hundred yards away. The two tents were closed but she opened the flaps and looked in. Neither of them was tidy, but although Jon's was in more of a muddle than David's there was no way of knowing whether a stranger had been interfering with them. There was an open one-inch map on Jon's sleeping-bag, and guessing that he would be annoyed at leaving it behind she picked it up before closing up the tents again.

Somehow she felt uneasy and suspicious. Although she could not see anybody, and although she did not have that uneasy feeling that she was being watched, she was sure that something was wrong. *There was something she ought to know.*

She stood still, unheeding the first heavy drops of rain, and suddenly, as quick as the lightning flashed, she knew the truth. She looked down again at the village and because she could not see the street, she realized that *it was impossible for Miss Wildblood or anyone else to see the caravan on the hill from the street itself.* It couldn't be done and they had been fooled by the Wildblood who wanted to be left alone with Harriet!

With an involuntary cry of fear, Peter raced down the hill as the storm broke. At last she saw the little garden gate of Venton's a few yards ahead.

In a few seconds, she would know whether her fears were justified. The side door was open. The kitchen was empty. So was the sitting-room. The door into the shop was open and Peter knew now that there was nobody there and that the house was empty.

She grabbed her raincoat and went out into the rain. She ran across the road to Miss Wildblood's cottage and tried the door. It was locked. She banged on it but there was no reply. For a moment she leaned against the door fighting against panic. She thought of her friends and specially of David and wondered what he would do. Then, as the thunder crashed again she knew what she had to do. First she must ask in the village shop whether the children or Miss Wildblood had been seen in the street. Next, reminded by the map found in Jon's tent and which she was still clutching, she knew that she must somehow go and find the others.

Some of her courage returned as she crossed the street to the shop. Two village women were gossiping with the proprietor.

"Good afternoon," she said. "I wonder if any of you have seen Miss Wildblood and two girls about twelve and ten. They've disappeared and Miss Wildblood isn't in her cottage."

The women glanced at each other but did not speak. The man behind the counter shrugged and said:

"Funny goings-on here, miss. Funny you don't know what's happening to your friends. That Amy Wildblood has just gone off with those two kids in a car. There was a car pulled up outside Venton's after driving up and down the street for a while. It came past here a while ago and I see Amy and what looked like those kids in it. Going fast it was. What car? What colour? What number? Who was driving it? How would I know, miss? Thought they were friends o' yours . . . Too many strangers about this place these days."

12. *Edith and Amy*

ONLY A FEW MINUTES after Peter had gone up to see whether there were any strangers near the caravan, Miss Wildblood, left with Mary and Harriet, began to fidget again.

"I've something in my cottage I want to show you girls," she said. "Something in the paper it was. I cut it out but I forgot to bring it so I'll just run over and get it. I don't suppose your friend will be long, but you two stay right here and I'll be back in a minute . . ."

As soon as the door was closed, Harriet put her feet carefully to the floor. "Well!" she said. "What do you think of that, Mary? Is she all right, do you think?"

Mary frowned. "I think she's a liar. She couldn't think of a better fib than that about the paper. She's gone to telephone again. If I hadn't promised to stay with you I'd go and spy on her again, but I'm sure that's where she is . . . How does your ankle feel now?"

Harriet put her weight first on the sound foot and then on the bandaged ankle.

"Not too bad. It just aches. There's somebody coming now, Mary!"

She sat down again as the door burst open and Miss Wildblood stumbled into the sitting-room. Her eyes were wild as she gasped:

"I hardly know how to tell you, Harriet, but just as I was crossing the road a car comes along and stops just outside. There's a man driving it, but a lady in the back leans out of the window and asks for your grandfather and if not, she wants to see you with a special message. I reckon she knew

Mr Sparrow in London. She won't tell me what it is and she won't come in."

Harriet put a hand on Mary's shoulder and hobbled to the door.

"I'll go and see her with Mary," she said. "I'm old enough to take messages for my grandfather. I know that he told lots of his friends and customers in London that he was coming to Yorkshire. I can manage with Mary's help, thank you, Miss Wildblood."

Mary hardly had time to realize what was happening as Miss Wildblood insisted on taking Harriet's other arm and hurried them out into the street. Harriet managed very well, and before the girls could say anything, Miss Wildblood opened the rear door of a car standing at the kerb.

"There you are, dearie!" she muttered in an odd, strangled sort of voice. "The lady's inside waiting for you." —and as Harriet, looking puzzled, leaned forward, Miss Wildblood pushed her into the car and then followed, dragging Mary in after her.

"Get on! Get on!" she screamed hysterically to the driver. "I told you there were two. I can't help it, can I? We'll have to bring them both. Get on!"

The man in the driving-seat had a cap pulled down almost over his eyes. As he started the car he looked back over his shoulder and snapped, "Shut up all of you!"

The car roared forward as the storm broke. A crash of thunder drowned Harriet's scream for help, while Mary fought and struggled with Miss Wildblood who was babbling some nonsense which they could not hear. Suddenly Mary saw the face of the driver in the mirror. It was Robens. They had all fallen into the trap so cleverly baited by the wily Amy Wildblood.

As the car's pace increased, the storm reached its full fury and the force of the rain almost stopped the windscreen wipers. Harriet screamed:

"Mary! Are you all right? Don't you *dare* to hurt her, you wicked, wicked woman. *Leave her alone.*"

The car skidded as Robens braked and splashed through a pool of water on the road and stopped. Robens turned round.

"Neither of the doors at the back are locked," he shouted above the roar of the rain on the roof. "Lock them by moving the handles over else some of you may fall out when I get going again . . . *Do as you're told, girls* . . . It's no use struggling and no good making a row. If you keep quiet you'll be all right." And the car started up again.

Mary tried to recognize some landmark and to find out where they were, but the windows were steamed up and although the rain was now no more than a steady downpour, all that she had been able to see was that they were rushing through narrow lanes and not across the moors. She was about to mention Peter but suddenly realized that to remind these two of her might be very unwise.

The car slowed down in a lane with trees on the left and some open country rolling downhill on the right. The storm had now passed and when Mary rubbed the mist from the window she saw a glimpse of blue, rain-washed sky. She had no idea where she was, nor of how many miles they had come, but doubted whether it was much more than twenty minutes since they had left Spaunton. They had certainly now to keep their wits about them and escape if they could.

Robens stopped the car opposite an old barn just off the road and passed the Wildblood a key. "Unlock the doors, Amy, and then stand aside as I drive in. Lock up after me. You two stay in the back. If you try to escape you're going to be hurt. And keep quiet."

Miss Wildblood took the key and, pushing in front of Harriet, opened the door of the car. "Do as you're told, dearies," she whispered. "Please don't get hurt. You're going to be all right if only you don't make a fuss."

Harriet looked at her shrewdly and then at Mary who shook her head. There did not seem much sense in trying to escape when they did not know where they were. Perhaps they would be able to find out more about their enemies if they stayed with them? As the door opened, Mary saw the big barn quite clearly. There were no other buildings near but a grassy cart-track ran downhill to the right beyond an old farm gate.

Amy, having unlocked and opened the doors of the barn, scrambled into the car again, and Robens drove into the gloom of the barn. He then got out and closed the doors behind him.

"Get out and behave yourselves," he snapped as he opened the car doors again. "If you're quiet and do as you're told you can wait in here. You can't get out unless I unlock the doors and if you shout I shall gag you both. I mean that."

There was enough light from two cobwebby windows high in the roof for the girls to see his face and they both realized that he meant it. He looked excited but ruthless, while Amy seemed so nervous and scared that she hardly knew what she was saying or doing.

Mary turned her back on them both.

"Don't speak to them, Harry. Don't have anything to do with them. They're bullies—an' I'm sure that they're criminals. Did you ever meet a real criminal before? My twin an' me think they're monstrous. I expect these two are really so frightened of us that they'll tie us up soon, so we might as well have a look round this smelly place first."

The barn reeked of oil and petrol. At the far end another shabby old car was parked and on a rough table was an oil-lantern and a few tools.

"Keep as far away from them both as we can," Mary said loudly and distinctly.

"I don't want to speak to them," Harriet agreed. "I never want to see them again but I can't walk far because of my ankle. I hurt it again in the car, Mary."

"Well, sit in this other car, then," Mary suggested, but Robens wouldn't have this. He had been standing with Amy close to the locked doors of the barn while watching the girls. Once they heard him say, "I tell you we're not to move from here until she comes," and after that they whispered so that their prisoners could not hear them. When Mary tried to open the door of the other car, however, Robens ran up the barn and pulled her back.

"Little fools," he snapped. "I'm trying to make things easy for you but you won't mind your own business. If you want to sit down go back to my car. And don't speak so loudly."

"Don't you *dare* to touch us again," Harriet said. "I'd like to sit down again, please, Mary, but I'll scream if that man touches me."

Robens then lit a cigarette and paced up and down the barn while the woman came over to them and whispered, "You mustn't be too hard on me, dearies. Amy never wanted to hurt you. Amy has to do whatever she's told."

"My grandfather, Mr Sparrow, didn't tell you to kidnap us and bully us," Harriet said coldly. "You're a liar and a traitor and a very, very wicked woman. It won't be long now before my grandfather comes to fetch us, and if you've got any sense you'll unlock those doors now and let us go. If you don't, I'm quite sure that he'll fetch the police, and then you'll be sorry anyway."

Miss Wildblood blinked at this and went over to Robens, now smoking furiously at the far end of the barn. They whispered together while Mary took her friend's hand. "That was wonderful, Harry. They really are worried. Are you scared?"

Harriet nodded and Mary went on, "So am I. But Peter will bring help, Harry—she'll tell the others and they'll find us somehow. I know she will."

"But why have they brought us here, Mary? All we know is that we're waiting for somebody to come. A 'she'. Who can it be?"

Before Mary could answer they heard a gentle knocking on the doors of the barn. Tap, tap, tap . . . Tap . . . Tap . . . Robens hurried to the door. With his head against it, the girls heard him whisper, "That you, Edith?"

"Yes. Yes," came the reply. "Let me in. Have you got the girl?"

As Robens opened the big doors and let in the evening sunlight, the two girls slipped out of the old car and looked at the newcomer. She too was untidy and wild-eyed with the same gipsy look about her as Amy Wildblood, and suddenly they realized that she was indeed another Wildblood and that these two eccentric women were sisters. Mary and Harriet shrank back against the car as Edith, with staring eyes, pointed a shaking finger at them.

"There's two of 'em," she babbled. "I can't take two. I was only told about one. I can't manage two of the little dears. It's a mistake to bring two. He said only one. I don't like what's going on here. Tell me what's happened, Amy. One of you kids will have to come with me. And you too, Amy."

Robens ran his nicotine-stained fingers through his hair and stood in front of the two girls as he answered the more eccentric of the Wildblood sisters.

"Calm down, Edith. Amy has messed up the arrangements and couldn't bring the young Sparrow without this other little nuisance. It can't be helped now, but I must get back. Now listen to me—"

The sisters having received their instructions, now approached the girls.

"Don't bother to speak to us," Mary said coldly. "We don't want to talk to you and we're coming without any fuss although you'll both be sorry for this. Just remember that my friend here has twisted her ankle and can't hurry. I shall help her and we hope we're not going far. Please don't touch us. We're not going to run away."

They turned at the sound of the engine of Robens' car and watched him as he backed out of the barn, got out and relocked the doors and then, before getting back into the car called out, "Don't stand there gaping. Get going, Amy, and don't be rough with them."

The two women opened the gate.

"Straight down the hill and keep to the track, dearies.

You're going to have a very exciting surprise."

The banks on each side of the track were steeper and higher as they went slowly down the hill with Mary helping Harriet not to put too much weight on her ankle.

The two girls walked a few paces behind the muttering sisters. Harriet stopped several times to rest and refused to be hurried. Presently they saw a pleasant valley below them and, on the opposite hillside, groups of trees and strange, grassy terraces and mounds. But these they hardly noticed because, to their surprise, they saw that their road crossed a single, rusty railway line by a bridge and that on the left, just before the bridge, were the ruins of a stone-built church standing in a wilderness which once must have been the graveyard.

Before the girls could discuss what they saw, the two sisters began to jabber excitedly and urge the children forward. "Hurry now. You must hurry. We'll help you now but you must be quick . . . We haven't got to walk much longer . . . You're going to have a lovely ride. Take her hand, Amy. Hurry now. Down the embankment. Down here."

Edith grabbed Mary and dragged her down a rough track to the railway line while Amy somehow got Harriet under an arm and stumbled down after her. On their left was the dark arch of the crumbling bridge, but right before them, on the rails, was a workmen's four-wheeled trolley.

"Get on that," Edith snapped. "Get on and hold tight. You too, Amy. Get the girl on first."

"I'm not going on that!" Amy shouted. "I won't do it. Why should I? I've done enough today. I'm going home."

By now Edith had taken control and the children were almost mesmerised by her and clung to each other on the trolley. Then she hauled her protesting sister on too and yelled, "Hold them on. We're going now"—and with these words she grasped the lever and worked it to and fro.

The wheels squeaked and then rumbled on the rusty rails. The lever clanked as Edith Wildblood increased the speed. Amy shouted and pointed ahead and the girls saw the dark, round mouth of a tunnel about fifty yards ahead. The single track was swallowed up in its blackness.

Harriet opened her mouth and screamed while Mary struggled out of her yellow cardigan and dropped it on the line as the trolley with its unusual cargo hurtled towards the tunnel and into the unknown.

13. The Link

PHILIP SHARMAN and the others stood at the edge of the Roman road and watched David, Peter and the two girls walk back towards the road.

"I'm sorry about Harriet," he said. "Perhaps we ought to have gone back together but I'm sure she's not badly hurt. Shall we go on slowly or wait for David here?"

Jon stood with his hands in his pockets and watched the others. Peter turned at the gate and waved and they all waved in reply. He was not feeling happy about what had happened. He realized why David had gone with the girls and he knew too that he was still suspicious of Sharman. There was so much about this young man that they did not know.

He turned to Penny who had always been so keen on this expedition.

"Let's go on, Jon," she said, "David will soon catch us up. If he isn't in sight by the time we get to the end of the road we'll wait for him there and have our elevenses."

So they went on, with Dickie and Macbeth a few yards ahead and Philip Sharman talking to Jon and Penny about archaeology.

The great rough stones showing above the surface of the turf disappeared about two hundred yards ahead. The road vanished as suddenly as it had begun—swallowed up by the moor.

Sharman explained.

"It goes on for miles, down to York. You can see the faint track from here and it's a grand walk but there are no more exposed stones. We'll wait here for David"—and he brought some chocolate from his pocket.

Soon they saw David on the horizon behind them and

Jon ambled back to meet him. When the former had explained about the others getting a lift to Goathland and that Harriet was certainly not any worse, they felt more cheerful and Penny said, "Of course we're very grateful to you, Philip. We know you've made up your mind to show us this deserted village. We know we've got to see it sometime, so shall we go now and get it over?"

Sharman unfolded his map and showed them where they were.

"We could follow the route of the old road for a while and then go down into the valley to the stream where three tracks meet. The centre path will then take us eventually to the hill on the slopes of which Coram Street was built. There's no real road leading directly to it now. Did I tell you that we were actually digging there in the summer and that I can show you the foundations of dwellings of several different generations? The weather is getting rather peculiar so perhaps we'll go the shorter way over the moor from here. There isn't a marked track but I can find the way. We shall save a mile and I'd like to get there as soon as I can now."

They were never quite sure why Sharman chose to take them this particular way to Coram Street. The weather became close and heavy, and after about half a mile Dickie was grumbling and David had to carry Macbeth who was not big enough to jump over the heather and soon became exhausted by burrowing through it. Certainly it would have been easier to use the track, although Sharman led them patiently and with good humour along the crest of rolling moorland which offered wonderful views. After an hour's walking they reached a cairn of stones and here they stopped to eat their sandwiches while Sharman got out his map again.

"What's the railway line marked on the map?" David asked as he looked over his shoulder. "Seems to run along the valley below Coram Street."

"It does. It's one of the many closed branch lines, but a few trains each day were running up to two years ago.

You'll enjoy it, Dickie, and although it's overgrown and rusty now you can walk along it. There's a tunnel too. See it on the map?"

"What's at the other end of the tunnel?" Penny asked.

"An old quarry," Sharman explained. "I don't remember when it was last worked, but I've been over the hill from Coram Street once and seen it. There's a row of deserted cottages there too. They must be in the loneliest place in Yorkshire."

They did not hurry. They talked about Harriet and the others and Sharman had plenty to tell them about his favourite subject, Yorkshire. Then, when none of them seemed suspicious, he questioned them cleverly about Mr Venton, Mr Sparrow, the shop and the old mine.

Although the answers he was given were evasive, David realized that Philip was mildly amused by them. He was sure, too, that it couldn't be long now before they asked each other some straight questions. It was ridiculous for there to be so much suspicion between them, and he looked up suddenly to see Sharman's eyes on him. He flushed because he was sure that the man knew what he was thinking, and, in an odd sort of way, he was glad that he did. He opened his mouth to speak but Sharman, with a shift of his eyes towards Penny who was watching them curiously, shook his head slightly.

"Come on," he said. "Time to be getting on. There's a track leading from this cairn to the hill above Coram Street so your dog can walk all the way now. See it, Dickie? You lead the way."

Half an hour later they left the moor and walked abreast down a grassy slope to a clump of hawthorn trees.

"You'll see Coram Street from there," Sharman said.

He led them down to the trees. Below them lay the forgotten valley and they could see the derelict railway line and a little stream beside it far below. Opposite was a hill, the sides of which were covered with bracken and across its slope, running gently down to the valley, was a grassy track.

"That's the Corpse Way," Sharman explained. "That

path has been there for hundreds of years, and until the old church fell out of use and was deconsecrated a hundred years or so ago, coffins were brought over that hill for burial from villages without a church. No easy job in winter either. None of you have seen snow in Yorkshire yet, but it can be as deep here as anywhere in the country. See how the Corpse Way runs down the side of the hill to the church? You can just see the tower above that clump of trees which hides a bridge over the railway."

"I thought you said there wasn't a road to this place," David said. "I can see a track leading up from behind those trees into another valley."

They followed his pointing finger and saw the dark stone tower of the old church to the right of this track under the slope of the hill. The Corpse Way led directly into the churchyard.

"That track is a very ancient road and leads up to a little used lane about three-quarters of a mile over the hill. It must have been the only road to the old village, but it isn't in use now. I've walked up it once. There's nothing much to see but plenty to imagine when you realize the age of that road."

"I thought we were going to see lots of exciting and ghostly old ruins," Dickie said with obvious disappointment. "What are all those sheets of rusty corrugated iron spread out on the grass down there?"

"I'll show you," Sharman said. "You can help me lift them and then you will see where we were digging in the summer. The iron sheets keep the rainwater out of the trenches that we have to dig to find the buried foundations of houses built on this spot hundreds of years ago. We find other things sometimes—coins, scraps of pottery and metal. Come and see before the storm breaks."

There was no doubt about Sharman's enthusiasm and, as with Penny and Dickie, he led the way down the hill, Jon whispered, "What do you make of him, David? He's keen enough on this, but why did he want us to come? Why does he waste his time on us and why those questions about old

Venton and Sparrow just now? He's sure that we know more than we tell him."

David slowed down and kept out of earshot.

"I know he is. I can't make it out, but somehow I think he's on our side, Jon. Come on! We'd better shelter in his trenches. Here comes the rain!"

The storm broke with a crash of thunder that rolled round the hills and down the valley. Lightning flashed and suddenly the horizon was blotted out by a grey curtain of rain.

They raced down the hill and helped Sharman and Penny who were struggling to lift one of the cumbersome sheets of corrugated iron. Dickie was shouting directions and dancing about in the rain, while Macbeth lifted up his black muzzle and howled. Jon and Sharman, the tallest of the party, managed at last to lift one end of the iron sheet from the wooden posts to which it had been wired and hold it up, while the others scrambled into the trenches which were four or five feet deep. Then they slid in after the others and crouched in the gloom at the bottom of the trench while the rain thundered on the roof and ran in muddy streams round their feet.

"I think I should be more comfortable outside in the rain," Penny yelled above the hubbub of the storm, while Dickie did all he could to comfort Mackie who was more frightened by thunder than of a hundred dogs ten times his size! Nobody answered her because Sharman was showing the boys the edges of some old tiles which he said were the foundations of an early dwelling on this site.

Then the rain stopped and they climbed out of their gloomy prison and stretched thankfully in the sun.

"How long ago did this place die?" Penny asked as she shook the rain from her hair. "Why does a place like this just give up? Was it dead and deserted when the railway came?"

"The railway came down the valley because that was the easy way to build it and was nothing to do with a ruined church and a few cottages for quarry workers," Sharman said. "We think Coram Street started to die at the time of the Black Death in 1370, but what makes it so interesting is its age before that. That's what I'm trying to show you. We'll get all the iron shelters off this dig now and see it properly."

Once again the boys helped him to expose this particular part of the site, but Penny soon got bored and sat down on the damp turf and with her chin on her cupped hands looked down into the valley. Her thoughts slipped away to the so very different country of the Kent and Sussex borders where she lived, and the windy, cobbled streets of Rye standing on its hill above the levels of Romney Marsh.

Then David jumped out of the trench and joined her.

"Getting bored, Penny? So am I. Dickie and Macbeth are playing some sort of hunting game and Jon is the only one really interested in these old ruins. Can you see what I see? There's actually another human being down there."

He pointed to the track leading beyond the trees at the bottom of the valley and Penny saw a woman hurrying up the hill in the direction of the church. She was too far away for them to see what she looked like so David called back to Sharman and asked for his binoculars. Penny stood beside him as he focused them on the stranger just before she disappeared round a turn in the sunken road past the church.

"Rum-looking woman," he said. "Looked a bit like a gipsy. Where's she come from, I wonder? Philip said that there's a bridge over the railway down there, didn't he? I know it's ridiculous but that woman reminds me of somebody and yet I don't think I've seen her before. I couldn't have done!"

He passed the glasses back to Sharman who with Jon had now climbed out of the workings. Dickie then handed Macbeth up and they all sat down on the grass together. Sharman lit his pipe and said, "Gipsy sort of woman, did you say? We used to see her wandering about the valley sometimes when we were digging here. No idea where she lives and she always seemed to want to avoid us."

"I'd like to know how the others are getting on," said Penny suddenly. "Shouldn't we all go back to Spaunton first, and then I think some of us should go to Pickering to meet Mr Sparrow?"

Sharman looked at his watch.

"Good idea. But we needn't start just yet. I've got something to say to all of you first, so please listen before we start back. Why don't you tell me the truth? I know that Mr Sparrow is being pressed to sell his property because there is something of value in the old mine. I think I know what it is and I'm sure he shouldn't sell. *Can't you see that I'm on your side?* Tell me what's happened."

"Why should we?" Jon asked quickly. "Are you a detective?"

Sharman laughed. "Not me! I'm a geologist interested in archaeology and I'm sure there are uranium deposits in that mine and a geiger counter would prove it. What's happened to that chap who was trespassing there?"

"Jon and I can tell you plenty about him—" Penny began, and then was interrupted by Dickie who pointed down the valley.

"Look!" he shouted. "There's somebody else running down the hill. It's a girl. It looks like Peter!"

They all jumped up and David snatched the binoculars from Sharman and after one quick look, passed them back and said, "I'm sure it's Peter and she looks in trouble. Please stay here unless I shout for you. I'll bring her up here soon as I can"—and he raced off.

Suddenly afraid, David pounded down the hill towards the clump of trees at the bottom of the valley by the railway. He could no longer see Peter nor the bridge over the line described by Sharman, and he wondered where she was going. His brief glimpse of her had scared him because she had looked frightened.

He stopped and shouted her name with what breath he had left and then, with his fingers in his mouth, he whistled the Lone Piners' signal—the two-note, haunting cry of the peewit. And as he listened, there came from the clump of trees a hundred yards below him, the faint and wavering reply.

"Coming, Peter!" he shouted and ran forward again. He saw her leaning against the trunk of a tree. Her hands were over her face and she did not look up when he called to her again. He felt a sudden stab of fear as he wondered why she was here alone and what had happened to the others.

He stopped a yard from her and gasped, "Hello, Pete. What's wrong?"

Only on a few occasions had he seen her anything but clean and fresh and well-groomed. She was that sort of girl. Now her bare, brown legs were scratched and blood-stained. Her cotton skirt was torn and muddy and her raincoat was torn. Her corn-coloured hair was untidy and he realized to his horror that she was sobbing.

Gently he lifted her hands from her face.

"It's me, Peter. David. We're all here. What's wrong? What's happened? Where are the others?"

"Oh, David," she whispered. "I've been saying a prayer all the time that I'd find you here. It won't be so bad now. I can't tell you how pleased I am to see you. Where are the others?"

He looked back over his shoulder and then realized that they could not see them.

"Up there on the hill, Pete. We'll go up in a minute. Tell me first what's happened?" He put his arm round her shoulders and she suddenly looked up at him.

"We've got to do something *quickly*, David. We must tell the police before Mr Sparrow comes back. I was tricked by Amy Wildblood and she's disappeared with Harriet and Mary. All I know is that they were taken off in a car from Spaunton. They've been kidnapped, David, and it's all my fault and nobody in that beastly village knew which way the car had gone . . . No, let me finish, David. I must tell you before the others know about it. She tricked me by telling us that she'd seen strangers round our caravan on the moor and when I got back the house was empty. She's not in her cottage and twice we saw her telephoning and she was most peculiar and excited. And I let it happen, David, and now they've got Mary as well as Harriet. I found Jon's map and remembered you were going to Coram Street and got a lift. Lend me a handkerchief then we'll find the others . . . Let me go now, David, please—and thank you for being here."

He did as she asked, then, "Follow me up the hill, Peter. I'll go ahead and tell them first. Don't worry. We'll soon find those two and nobody will dare to hurt them. Philip Sharman has just told us that he's on our side. I wondered if he was a detective but he says he isn't. Here's Dickie. You speak to him while I tell the others."

She blew her nose loudly and gave him a shaky smile. "Better now. Thanks, David. Always about when you're wanted, aren't you?"

He ran back out of the shadow of the trees and was stopped by Dickie and Macbeth.

"What's happened?" the former demanded. "Where's my twin? I know something has happened and you've got to tell me, David. I was sure something was going to happen . . . *Where's Mary?*"

"She'll be all right. Peter will tell you all about it. Tell her not to worry, Dickie. Make a fuss of her. Lone Piners stick together."

Dickie's lower lip had looked shaky but he gave his brother a shrewd look before running on to meet Peter.

Ten minutes later Philip Sharman had taken control and was leading them as quickly as they could walk along the Corpse Way. As soon as David had told them Peter's story, Jon told him about the "Doctor" and Robens in Whitby and of their now justified suspicion of Amy Wildblood. To save time Philip had led them straight down into the valley into the railway cutting and up the other side of the hill until they struck the ancient track.

"You've certainly let yourselves in for something," he said as they panted up the steep hillside. "It's worse than I thought. Of course the police must be told, but I'm sure the first thing to do is to get to Pickering and meet Mr Sparrow. He must be told everything at once. If we're lucky and get a lift on the main road we can get to the station on time. If we're likely to be late we'll telephone the station and ask him to wait for us and we'll contact the police as well. This is the quickest way, but we've got to move fast."

And so they hurried over the shoulder of the hill and down the other side for half a mile or more until the old track crossed the new road on which they hoped to get a lift to Pickering. It was now twelve minutes to six and Sharman, looking at the map as he hurried along, saw that the nearest telephone kiosk was nearly a mile farther on. He was about to ask David or Jon if one of them would run ahead and get a message through to the railway station when a car came up behind them and the girls waved frantically. Luckily it was a large, old-fashioned car with room for them all and the driver a grey-haired lady in tweeds.

Philip Sharman exerted his charm and the Lone Piners were put down just outside Pickering station as the train arrived. They crowded into the booking-hall just as the few passengers came out and to their surprise they heard the ticket collector saying, "Mr Sparrow, please. Message for Mr Sparrow."

Then they saw Mr Sparrow with a little gnome-like man with a rosy face, a brown overcoat and a green felt hat. The former spoke to the ticket collector who passed him a long envelope and then he saw the Lone Piners waiting for him. As they crowded round he seemed to sense that something was wrong.

"How good of you to meet me. This is my friend, Mr Venton. But why have you come and where is Harriet?"

David turned quickly to Peter.

"Philip and I will explain. We can't talk here so please wait for us outside. Don't worry, Peter. He'll understand."

Philip nodded agreement. "I saw a garage on the corner. See if they've two cars for hire because I'm sure we must get back to Spaunton as soon as we can. Don't let anybody else know of our troubles yet."

It was dusk when the cars pulled up outside Venton's. Sharman was the first to get out and the others watched him run across the road to Amy Wildblood's cottage. There was no light in the windows and the door was locked and he was back just as the others were crowding into Venton's and switching on the lights. There was nobody there. No message. Nothing seemed to have been disturbed.

"We are all grateful for your help, Mr Sharman," said Mr Sparrow. "Please telephone the police at once and ask them to send someone here immediately. I blame myself for not taking action more quickly."

"And keep courage up," Mr Venton said unexpectedly in rather a squeaky voice. "This is all disgraceful and I've been a fool. Should have been more suspicious when all this started. Better tell them about that impertinent letter, Sparrow."

"Very well. Sit down, my dears."

They could hear the murmur of Philip's voice on the telephone in the shop as Mr Sparrow told them about the letter which had been left for him at Pickering station.

"It is a threatening and unpleasant letter. It was marked 'Confidential and Urgent' and although it is unsigned I think we know who wrote it. I'm sorry to tell you that it states that Harriet and Mary will not be returned unless I agree to sell my property immediately. A document for me to sign was enclosed and I am to make my decision by the morning at latest."

"Who are you to tell of your decision?" Jon asked. "Is there an address on the letter?"

"No, Jonathan. No address. Our enemies are very clever. If I agree to sell—and obviously they believe that I shall—I am to move the old French clock which you have all seen in the centre of the shop window to the right-hand side."

"You're to move the clock? Who will see it? Surely we've only to watch carefully to see who comes up and down the street in the morning," David said.

"In the morning?" Peter cried. "We can't wait till the morning to get the girls back. They must be found at once. What good are the police if they can't find them tonight? Who delivered the note at the station?"

"They didn't know, my dear. They said they didn't notice, but it hadn't been waiting for me very long and whoever left it knew that I should be on the London train."

"Witch Wildblood, of course!" Dickie shouted with a catch in his voice. "Witch and traytress."

Sharman came back into the room.

"I've described the 'Doctor', and Robens and Amy, and told them about Harry and Mary. There's a police patrol car not far away and it should be here in five minutes."

It was, and everybody was thankful to break the tension of waiting. Mr Sparrow took control and with Mr Venton's help told them about the anonymous offers for the business and of what they knew of the "Doctor", of Robens and of Amy Wildblood. They were impressed by the letter left for him at Pickering station.

Then Sharman tried to speak but was interrupted by Peter and Dickie and because the latter would not be shouted down they had to listen to him first.

"Why do you keep on talk, talk, talk," he said with tears in his eyes. "There you are with a whacking great car outside and a radio and you don't go an' find my twin and Harriet. Can't you jolly well see they've been kidnapped? We keep telling you an' all you do is write in a notebook and look at us as if we're all liars—"

"Richard!" Mr Sparrow warned. "Please be quiet. There is no need to be rude."

"Yes there is!" Dickie shouted. "Yes there is. We've got to find Mary and Harry, haven't we? How do we know they're not being tortured? They're trusting us, and now we've got these policemen an' their cars an' things an' what do they do—?"

"Hi!" the younger of the two policemen interrupted. "That's enough of that, young man. Who's talking now?" —and he lifted Dickie and swung him on to the table so that he was looking down on all of them. "Stop bullying us. We'll find your girls. Nobody will dare hurt them."

Dickie sniffed as the other policeman inquired, "This man you call the 'Doctor' now? The man you think is behind all this. Have you any suggestions as to where he may be staying or where he might have taken the children?"

"Yes," Penny said quickly. "The man Robens had rooms over a horrid little tobacco shop in Prospect Way, Whitby. You don't give us time to tell you but they tried to keep me there once . . . It's true."

"O.K.," the senior policeman said to his companion. "Contact Whitby, George, and ask them to have a look. Tobacconist's shop in Prospect Way."

"Tell them to ask if Mr Warner is still there," Penny said. "That's the name Robens was using then."

The younger policeman swung Dickie to the ground. "Come and help me son," he said. "You're the sort of chap we want in the Force"—and Dickie went with him as if he were already a detective.

Then Jon spoke up.

"Of course we can't be sure, but I don't think the 'Doctor' is far away. He met Robens in Whitby as Penny knows. He also met him on Goathland station. We know that he's probably looking all over Yorkshire for old mine workings and searching them for deposits of uranium."

"So that's the racket?" the policeman said. "What's he going to do with a mine when he gets it?"

"Sell it to the Ministry of Fuel and Power, of course," Sharman snapped. "The Government has said they'll help private owners who may have uranium on their land. That's what this man is doing. He's buying up land with uranium on it and will then re-sell it at a tremendous profit."

David suddenly clapped his hands to his forehead.

"I've got a brainwave!" he shouted. "When we were at Coram Street this afternoon I saw a strange woman. I looked at her through Philip's glasses and she reminded me of somebody. I've been puzzling this out and now I'm sure that she reminded me of our Amy Wildblood. The two could be sisters. Suppose they are? Suppose they've been working together on this? We know that Amy knew Robens. We know that Amy did a lot of telephoning this afternoon after Peter and the girls got back here. Suppose Amy reported to the 'Doctor' that they'd come back unexpectedly? Peter has told us how Amy kept on trying to get rid of her and how Mary refused to leave Harriet. Isn't there a chance that the 'Doctor' is hiding somewhere near Coram Street and the woman I saw is working for him with Amy and Robens? I bet the woman I saw is the link. See what I mean?"

Dickie had come back into the room and heard David's deductions.

"Come on then!" he shouted. "Let's go back to Coram Street. Mackie will find them. Take torches an' things and hunt them out. Don't you worry any more, Mr Sparrow. We'll find them. Up the Lone Piners!"

14. *The Fire*

AS THE TROLLEY carrying the Wildbloods with Mary and Harriet, rumbled with increasing speed towards the tunnel's mouth the two girls clung fearfully to each other. Amy's scream was cut short, like an engine's whistle, when it hurtled into the darkness and Edith, working frantically at the lever, shouted over her shoulder, "Hold tight, dearies. Hold tight! Don't rock the boat, dearies!"

The wheels screeched on the rusty rails, the lever clanked, and the echoes of this din, together with Amy's renewed screams beat back deafeningly from the dripping walls. The air was cold, and horrid drops of water fell from the roof as they hurtled forward on their nightmare journey.

The chill struck through Mary's thin dress and her teeth chattered as Harriet held her close and shouted in her ear, "Where are they taking us, Mary? This can't last for ever, can it? *I want it to stop!*"

But it did not stop. It went faster and at last Amy's screams became whimpers and Edith stopped working the lever.

"She runs free now!" she shouted in triumph. "See how she runs! She's a beauty. What are you fussing about, Amy? I forgot you hadn't been this way before. We've got a cosy little place here. Ever so cosy. You'll like it."

While she was speaking Mary saw far in front of them a tiny, white pin-point of light. It got bigger, bigger, bigger. The air smelled cleaner. Suddenly the noise of the trolley changed as they rattled into the daylight.

"Sit still!" Edith shouted. "Do as you're told and you won't come to no harm. We're slowing down now."

Ahead, on the right of the railway track, the girls saw a row of cottages. From the chimney of the nearest rose a wisp of smoke. The trolley slowed to a stop opposite a path leading over waste ground to the door of this cottage.

"Off you get, dearies," Edith said. "Keep close to them, Amy, and see they don't try any funny capers. No doubt his lordship has seen us and he don't like being kept waiting. Are you two coming quietly?"

"Yes, we are," Mary said coldly. "But you needn't think that's because we're afraid of either of you or of anyone else. We utterly despise you."

"Our friends will find us soon," Harriet added. "They'll know where to find us too because of certain clues. You dare not hurt us. We've done nothing wrong, but you're the ones who are going to be sorry."

The women glanced at each other uneasily and then Edith hurried ahead. The girls followed but their spirits fell when they had a closer look at the place to which they were being taken. Mary kept her thoughts to herself as Edith opened the door of the cottage, but she suspected who the man she had called "his lordship" might be. She did not like the idea of being kept a prisoner by the "Doctor" who would not be likely to forget some of their previous meetings.

"No fuss now!" Edith hissed as she grabbed Harriet's arm. "Just come quietly. The other one, too, Amy."

The girls just had time to see that they were in a narrow passage with a closed door on their left and a steep staircase on their right. There were two more doors at the end of the passage and that on the right, which was open, led into a kitchen. Edith opened the other door and pushed the girls into a small room.

There was not much to see. It was crowded with a lot of shabby furniture. The window, overlooking an overgrown yard behind the house, was small and the room was dim and stuffy.

"Stay there and be quiet and you won't be hurt," Edith said as she closed the door, and then Mary ran across in time to hear her muttering:

"Chair out of the kitchen. Quick, Amy. There's no key

for this lock. Wedge the door. Top of the chair under the handle."

Mary beckoned to Harriet and then tried the door. It was not quite closed but it was certainly tightly wedged, and although the handle turned the chair held it firmly. There was, however, a crack through which they heard first the two Wildbloods arguing and then the angry interruption of a man who must have come out of the front room.

"Stop that row!" he shouted. "What are you doing here, Amy, and why are there two children? You've got the Sparrow girl, haven't you?"

"Oh yes, sir. She's there but I had to bring the other because she wouldn't leave Harriet. I didn't want to make trouble, sir. They've been very good and it seemed better to bring both when the chance came, sir. It's been very, very difficult."

"So you've messed it all up, have you, Amy?" the man's voice cut in. "I told you and Robens to bring the Sparrow child only. You two go into the kitchen and shut the door. I'll see these youngsters and then tell you what I'm going to do."

There was a scuffle of feet in the passage and Mary dragged Harriet away from the door and sat with her in the old easy chair. "Don't show him that we're afraid, Harry. He can't really hurt us, and you know that I dropped my cardigan outside the tunnel?"

Then the door was wrenched open and a man came into the room. It was nearly dark, but the girls could see him more clearly than he could see them with their faces in the shadow. Mary recognized him at once. He was the man they knew as the "Doctor".

He crossed the room and looked down at them.

"Get up," he said quietly. "Turn to the window. I want to see you. Which of you is the Sparrow girl?"

"I am," Harriet said as she stood up. "Who are you? Please let us go at once."

"I can't do that yet," the "Doctor" said. "You'll have to stay in this house for a while, but I'll send you upstairs to a more comfortable room. There's nothing for you to worry about if you behave yourselves. What's your name, girl? You. The Sparrow child."

"Harriet," she said. "But I don't see what it's got to do with you. You *must* let us go. My grandfather will be very, very angry with you when he finds us."

"Ah! Your grandfather. Yes, indeed he may be angry. I'm glad you reminded me of him. I may ask you to write him a little note presently. I'm sure he'd like to hear from you, particularly as you will be spending the night here."

"But you can't do that!" Mary whispered. "We're not going to stay in this horrible house."

"Now let me look at *you*," the "Doctor" said in his horrid, silky voice. "You're the child who got in the way and insisted on coming too. How very foolish . . . Ah, yes. You are one of the nuisance children and I remember you on Goathland platform. Very impertinent. A night here will be quite a change for you. Don't try me too far."

Although there was quiet menace in these words and Mary was certainly frightened, she felt that the "Doctor" was really unsure of himself.

Harriet asked, "Why do you say that I might have to write to my grandfather? Where is he? Is there anything wrong—with him, I mean?"

"Nothing—yet," he sneered, and then opening the door he called, "Edith. Take these two upstairs into the front room. They're to be locked in, but you can give them what they want to eat and drink and just remember that you're responsible for them. Go on, you two, and no nonsense."

They had no choice. Even if they were able to escape from the house it was nearly dark and they had no idea where to go. The man pushed them into the hall where the two Wildbloods were waiting and they were taken upstairs. The room into which they were put was a bedroom with a single bed, a cane-seated chair, a hideous wash-stand and a small table under a window. There was only just enough light for them to see the two women when Mary said, "You are both very, very wicked women, and if you don't want to get into trouble you must take us away from here back to Spaunton. Mr Sparrow and our friends will be very angry about this. And we want a light. We can't stay here in the dark. *You fetch us a light quickly 'cos if you don't we shall scream and smash up the place.*"

Amy came across the room.

"Don't talk so loud, dearie. Don't make *him* angry. Please don't do that. You'll be all right if you'll be good. We'll get you a candle and a nice supper. What would you like for your suppers?"

"They'll get what I give 'em," Edith snapped. "Stop talking like a fool, Amy. Here they are and here they'll stay until he says they can go. Come along"—and she pushed her sister out of the room and locked the door on the outside.

For a moment the girls said nothing and then Harriet flung herself face down on the bed and began to cry. Mary was near to tears herself, but she really did have faith in her friends and was determined to make herself a nuisance to their enemies if she could. But it would be difficult if Harriet gave up.

She sat on the bed.

"Please don't cry, Harry. I feel like it too, but they mustn't know that we're scared of them. I was wondering whether we could frighten them enough to make them take us away. I'm sure Amy doesn't really want to hurt us. Don't cry, Harry. You're older than me and we must be brave because of the others and the Club—"

"I'm not really a member of your silly old club," Harriet gulped. "I do everything with you but I'm still not a real member and anyway I'm as brave as you. It's just that I'm so worried about my grandfather, Mary."

"I understand Harry. I know why you're so miserable about him. You mean that when he gets home you won't be there and somebody will have to tell him? But Peter knows that it was Amy who got us away. So try not to worry Harry, they'll find us."

Harriet sat up, fumbled unsuccessfully for a handkerchief and then dabbed her eyes with the hem of her dress.

"All right, Mary. I won't cry again. I'm sorry. There is one thing—my ankle is much stronger now, so if there's a chance to escape . . . I wish they'd bring us a light. And I'm hungry too."

Mary went over to the window.

"It's easier to see out if there isn't a light in the room," she said. "P'raps we could signal to somebody."

The window was small and dirty and the catch was so rusted that it was impossible to open it.

"I s'pose we could smash it with the chair," Harriet said. "But it's too far from the ground for us to jump. Let's first make a noise on the door and make them bring us a light."

Mary agreed and started to kick and bang on the door with her fists.

"Bring us a light!" she yelled. "Bring us something to eat! Let us out! Let us out! Bring us a LIGHT!"

Harriet took up the refrain and added rather obviously, "We hate you all! We loathe you beastly witches." And when she stopped for a moment they heard the telephone ringing downstairs and the "Doctor" shouting for quiet.

"Now jump on the floor," Mary gasped. "I hope the ceiling falls down and it will be difficult for him to hear what someone is trying to tell him."

She jumped on the floor and Harriet banged a chair. Down below the "Doctor" roared louder and louder and the two Wildbloods seemed to be screaming. One of the legs snapped off Harriet's chair just as their door was unlocked and flung back and the two women rushed in.

Harriet held the chair in front of her and Mary snatched up the broken leg and whirled it round her head. It was as well that she did so for Edith Wildblood rushed at them.

"Be quiet! Be quiet!" she screeched. "If you carry on like this we'll tie you up. He's so angry that he'll come up and beat you if you don't behave yourselves."

"Oh no he won't," Mary said. "He'd be afraid. You're the ones he'll be angry with. Why didn't you bring us a light? Why don't you bring us something to eat? We're not going to sit in the dark. You just do as we say else we'll make a noise again and say that you're not looking after us properly. And please hurry up."

The two women stared at them, and in the silence that followed Mary's outburst they heard the rumble of the "Doctor's" voice downstairs as he spoke on the telephone. Then Harriet put down the chair and, taking courage from Mary, said, "If you come any nearer I'll jab you with this. Go and get a light."

Without turning round, Edith said to Amy who was standing with her back to the closed door, "Get a candle, Amy. And matches."

"Dunno where they're kept. I'm not going. It's your kitchen, so you get them. Lock the door after you."

After some muttering and grumbling Edith did this and the girls were left alone with Amy. As soon as the door was locked she stepped forward and began to plead with them.

"Please do as I say, dearies. Please listen to me. Don't make them angry downstairs. I don't want you to get hurt."

"You're afraid," Mary said shrewdly. "You're afraid that you're going to be found out. And you *will* be found out too. Why don't you help us to escape and come with us and then we'll tell Mr Sparrow that you were kind to us? Do you know where this place is, Amy? Have you been here before?"

"Quiet, quiet!" the woman whispered. "You mustn't talk like that. You don't understand. It's very difficult for Amy. You just do as you're told now and it will be better for you. That's the thing for you to do. Hush now!"

The girls were sure that she was wavering, but at that moment the lock clicked back and the door opened suddenly. The "Doctor" was on the threshold with Edith behind him.

"And what are you whispering about, Amy?" he asked. "You wouldn't be having any silly ideas of how these children are to be treated, would you? They should not have been left without a light, and they are to have a good meal and that's all. Don't talk to them. And there'll be trouble for you two girls if you make any more noise. You're staying here tonight so you'd better make the best of it."

He nodded and turned away while Edith put two lighted candles on the wash-stand. Then their three gaolers went out and re-locked the door. Ten minutes later the women reappeared with their food—meat out of a tin, bread, butter and cheese, a banana and two mugs of cocoa.

"If you've got any sense you'll eat that lot and get off to bed," Edith said. "There's nothing wrong with it."

"Make the best of it, dearies," Amy twittered. "Everything will be all right in the morning"—and the two Wildbloods went out and the girls heard the lock click again.

They ate quickly because they were hungry, but had not much to say to each other. Harriet could not forget her grandfather, and in spite of Mary's example she was frightened and was sure she would show her fear if she spoke. Mary's courage was waning, too. She was now so tired that she could hardly keep her eyes open. From below they heard the rumble of the "Doctor's" voice and twice the telephone rang.

"Do you think the others will find us?" asked Harriet. "Tonight, I mean. Will they come, Mary? P'raps one of us ought to watch from the window all the time. If we see them we shall have to smash the window."

Mary agreed but realized that she could not keep awake much longer.

"We'll have a little sleep first, Harry. We'll feel better when we've had a rest."

And so, as the full moon slid up the sky outside and the flames of the candles burned steadily like golden spear-points the girls, frightened, exhausted and grubby, forgot their misery for a while in sleep.

* * * * *

But there was no sleep for the trio downstairs. The

quarrelling began when the "Doctor" called the Wildbloods into his room and nagged them for bringing two girls instead of one. He strode nervously up and down the room and when either of the women tried to speak he shouted them down.

"And you're a fool, Edith. You took much too long over the job and then you should have taken those candles up earlier. We don't want to scare them too much—yet. Neither of you have got any sense and I don't know why I bother with you. You're well paid and do precious little for it. Remember that you're responsible for those children upstairs. Either of them has got more sense than both of you. Now I'm hungry so you'd better get me something to eat. I fancy bacon. And two fried eggs and tomatoes."

While he was speaking the two women glanced at each other meaningly.

"There aren't any tomatoes," Edith said firmly. "If you want tomatoes you must get them yourself. You can fry your own bacon too. Amy and me don't like this business. It's gone too far—"

"Yes it has," her sister broke in. "It's not right to do this sort of thing to these children. Edith and me have had enough of it. Let them go. There'll be trouble—"

"TROUBLE!" he roared. "There's going to be trouble all right. You two gone mad? I'll deal with you in a minute, Edith, after I've told Amy what she does next. I've just been trying to tell you that you've got no sense. Can't you see that you're the one who kidnapped two children this afternoon? You did it and nobody else and if there's ever any trouble you're responsible. Surely you can see that? And Edith helped you. Edith is responsible too."

"But you give me your orders!" Amy shouted. "You and Robbie are the ones. Not me. Nor Edith."

Before the "Doctor" could answer they heard the sound of hurrying footsteps on the path outside, and then a crash as the door was slammed and Robens stormed into the room.

"What are you doing here?" the "Doctor" shouted. "I

told you to stay away until I telephoned. Anything gone wrong? And what's the matter with you anyway? You're looking pleased with yourself."

Robens lit his cigarette and spoke first to the two women.

"You look as if you've all been having a nice happy little party. Are those two girls all right?"

Amy nodded. "Yes, yes. Good as gold now. No trouble. They're up in their room nice and cosy and they've had their supper."

"Why have you come?" demanded the "Doctor". "You're disobeying orders."

"Maybe I am and I'll tell you why I'm here, and you two Wildbloods may as well stay and hear what I've got to say. I'm tired of being ordered around over this business. I've done all the work for you, Doc, and now I'm certain that you've wasted it. This kidnapping of two young children won't do. It's too dangerous a game to play, and they should be taken home at once before the police get on to us. Your plan can't work, Doc, and even if old man Sparrow signed that paper I'm sure you'd never be able to hold him to it. You can do as you like but I'm clearing out. I'm advising you to let me take those two girls back to Spaunton before this hide-out is found. Why don't you—"

But he said no more because the "Doctor", speechless with rage, sprang at him, and the two, grunting and swearing, struggled together. The women shrank back against the door as the "Doctor" flung Robens against the rickety table and sent the oil-lamp crashing to the floor. It was an old-fashioned lamp with a thick glass container, but it fell on to the fender and broke. In a second the running oil burst into flames as the two men grappled. The flames caught a newspaper which flared up and spread the fire to the table-cloth. Robens, in such a rage now that he hardly noticed the spreading fire, forced the "Doctor" back into a corner and sent him crashing to the floor with a blow to the chin.

At this the Wildbloods, in a panic, fled out of the house and ran as far as the railway line. Edith was about to suggest that they should both escape on the trolley, but before she could speak, Amy screamed. The mouth of the tunnel was in black shadow, but about fifty yards from where they were standing there was a silver pool of moonlight almost as bright as day. And as they watched, a crowd of people ran from the darkness into the light.

"They've found us!" Amy screamed. "They're all here. Get on the trolley and force it through them. Get on!"

But they were too late. The Lone Piners were on the trail and were too angry to care what they did. The Wildbloods were recognizable in the moonlight, and with a shout of triumph they dashed towards them. David and Peter—the latter carrying Mary's yellow cardigan—were in the lead and had their eyes on the two women. So it was Penny running up next who first saw the flicker of flames behind the window of the cottage.

"Fire!" she shouted. "The place is on fire!" and then there came a crash of breaking glass as the window was broken and flames leaped out. Amy Wildblood had her hands over her eyes but Peter tore them away.

"Where are they, Amy? Tell us. Now. Are Mary and Harriet in that house?"

"Yes, yes, dearie. In the upstairs room. It wasn't my fault. Amy never did it. It's those men. They made me."

Philip Sharman and Jon came up just as the "Doctor", hotly pursued by Robens, dashed out of the burning house.

"David and Jon with me!" Sharman shouted. "Get the girls out first. The police will look after the men."

The "Doctor" dashed off to the left towards the quarry as soon as he saw the Lone Piners running towards him, but Robens, still in hot pursuit, was not as quick as Macbeth. Peter, Penny and Dickie all had the same idea at the same time, but it was the latter who sent the frenzied little dog in pursuit of their old enemy. As Sharman and the boys were forced back from the open door of the cottage by the roaring flames, Macbeth had driven the breathless, battered and cursing "Doctor" into the pool in the quarry.

* * * * *

Upstairs in their grubby room, Mary and Harriet slept through the fight between the two men but were wakened by the crackle of the hungry flames. Mary woke first, and as she sat up trying to remember where she was, she sniffed the awful smell of fire. For a moment she was speechless with fright and then she shook Harriet awake and dragged her off the bed.

"The house is on fire, Harry! Try the door."

Harriet, still half asleep, stumbled across the room but the door was still locked. The wooden panels were warm to the touch and her nose tingled with the sharp tang of smoke.

"Smash the window out with the chair," she shouted to Mary. "We'll have to jump."

Out clattered the glass and then Mary stood on the chair so that she could see out. Below her were David, Jon, and Philip Sharman shouting at her.

"If there's any bedding in the room, throw it out. Everything. You'll have to jump but we'll catch you. Hurry. We can't get up the stairs to you. Hurry, Mary."

The girls tore off counterpane, sheets and blankets and ran back to the window.

"Blankets first," Sharman shouted. "We'll catch you in a blanket. Can you manage to jump clear of the window? One at a time."

Down went three blankets and then Harriet, looking out of the window, wondered whether she would find the courage to jump. She watched Sharman, Jon, David and Peter each take a corner of the blanket while behind her Mary could now smell the paint blistering on the door.

"You first, Mary," Harriet said as she stepped off the chair. "You're the youngest. Be brave and show me the way."

Harriet helped Mary to sit on the window-sill which was not really very far from the ground. Mary felt a moment's panic, and then looking down at the faces of those she loved and trusted, she saw her twin jumping with excitement a few yards away and Philip Sharman looking up at her.

"Now, Mary," he called. "Jump now, poppet," and she was so surprised to hear what he called her that she held her breath, jumped, bounced in the blanket and found herself being hugged by Penny and unexpectedly kissed by Peter. Almost before she had recovered her breath Harriet was beside her and they were all running back towards the railway line.

After that everything happened so quickly that none of them, afterwards, were sure of the order of events. They remembered Amy Wildblood rushing at them hysterically and Edith standing moodily by the trolley as Mr Sparrow, Mr Venton and two policemen came out of the tunnel into the moonlight. Philip, knowing now that all the Lone Piners were safe, ran to meet the four men, and then a wet, muddy and bedraggled Mackie came trotting proudly up to the twins. Mary fell on him joyfully and found that, clenched in his jaws, was a piece of dark cloth which later was identified as part of the "Doctor's" trousers.

Mr Venton, who was older than Mr Sparrow, was exhausted by his journey through the tunnel but the latter, with tears on his cheeks, refused to be parted from Harriet who clung to his hand.

It was David who first realized that they had all forgotten about the "Doctor" and Robens and so, by the light of the flames from the burning cottage, Jon, David, Sharman and one of the policemen searched the quarry. There was no sign of either of the men, so it was assumed that they had escaped in the confusion.

"They can't get far," the policeman said as they returned to the others.

"He's got a car in the old barn up by the lane," Harriet reminded them. "And Robens has got a car too."

"We've got two cars and a man up there ourselves, miss," the other policeman smiled. "It's time you were all back in your beds, I'm thinking. I wouldn't have believed it was possible for so many kids to be mixed up with so much trouble. We'll get back to the cars now, and it will be quicker if we use this trolley to get you all through the tunnel although it will mean several trips. There's nothing we can do about the fire. It must burn itself out."

Jon and David volunteered to take the twins, Harriet, Penny and Mackie through first, and then Jon would take it back for the next load. Just as the first party was climbing on, a tall man walked out of the shadows on the other side of the line. It was Robens and they heard him say to the policemen, "I'll come along with you. Plenty to tell you. The 'Doctor' is away somewhere but he'll have had enough by the morning." Then he strolled over to the trolley and spoke directly to Penny, Harriet and Mary.

"I'm sorry," he said. "He tried to push me over the edge of the quarry, and then I remembered that you two were still in there so I came back." He turned to David and Jon. "You can all be proud of those two girls and of the red-head, too. Maybe I wouldn't be in this mess now if I'd had their courage. Cheerio!"—and he walked back to the police officers waiting for him.

* * * * *

Although so much had happened in this one fabulous day, as Dickie called it, all the Lone Piners, with Mr Sparrow, Mr Venton and Philip Sharman were back in Spaunton before ten o'clock. Police cars had been at their service and they had been taken home before Robens and the Wildbloods had gone off to Pickering Police Station.

They were all desperately tired but the Lone Piners refused to go to bed until they had talked everything over. So everyone settled down with enormous mugs of cocoa, cheese, biscuits and cake to go through their adventure again.

Penny, sitting on a cushion on the floor next to Jon, looked up at Sharman and smiled.

"We're sorry we were suspicious of you, but you were suspicious of us, weren't you?"

"Perhaps. I wondered for a time what you were all up to," he laughed. "There were so many of you that you were rather bewildering. I was suspicious of Robens—or Warner as he called himself then—at once. As soon as I saw the equipment he was so anxious to keep close to him I was sure that he'd got what is called a Scintillation Counter. I expect Jon knows as much about those as I do."

"Of course I don't," Jon said. "I read somewhere that although they were originally used only for the detection of uranium-bearing ores they're now used for oil exploration as well. You know how I checked in the Whitby Library and found the article in the papers about the search in this country—particularly in the north—for uranium. It said that the Atomic Energy Authority will help private prospectors and even members of the public to test anything which might be radio-active. I wanted to be sure of all that before we told Mr Sparrow of our suspicions, but we left it too late."

"Not at all, my boy," Mr Sparrow beamed. "You have all been extremely intelligent and proved yourselves to be loyal friends. I think you should know that Mr Venton and I have agreed to share anything of value which may be found in the mine and it seems possible that we shall be fortunate. Whatever happens, you will all be welcome here in Spaunton at any time."

"There's a thing I'd like to do before we have to go back," Dickie said as he smothered a yawn. "I'd like to see that deserted village again and have a whole day working that super trolley. It's a most fabulous thing."

"There's always tomorrow," Penny laughed as she got up. "The holiday isn't over and lots may happen yet. Let's go to bed now. Harriet is yawning and Mary's nearly asleep."

Mr Sparrow said he would walk down to the inn with Mr Venton and Philip so the Lone Piners went to see them off.

"See you all tomorrow, and thank you for quite a rousing day," Philip smiled.

"Good night and thank you all," said Mr Venton.

Harriet ran over and kissed Mr Sparrow and then they stood watching the three men as they walked down the hill.

Philip turned and raised his arm and they waved back.

"He's nice," Peter said as she slipped her arm into David's. "We do meet some nice people and what a lot has happened since we all squabbled about coming up here. Let's all walk a little way up the moor and then get to bed before Mr Sparrow comes back."

So they all trudged through the garden and up on to the moor where the roof of the girls' caravan was gleaming in the moonlight.

Then a big white owl sailed silently over their heads.

"Just like Witchend," Peter whispered. "I never hear an owl without remembering how we all started the Lone Piners. You must come there with us soon, Harry. You belong to us now. Good night now."

The twins and Harriet, with Mackie gambolling between them, ran down to the house and when they were in the sitting-room Dickie said, "Tell you what, you two. Wish I'd been with you in that smelly old cottage."

"So do we," Harriet said. "We didn't tell the others, Dickie, but we were absolutely terrified. We'll tell you every word about it tomorrow, but there's still one thing I want you to do before we go to bed. *Please?* . . . I know I'm supposed to be a member of the Club at last, but will you both sign a special paper for me now just to prove that I am? I want it *now*. Tonight, this very minute."

"We jolly well will," Dickie said. "You find a piece of paper, Harry, and you get a needle, Mary. I've got a ball-point pen in my pocket somewhere.

It took longer to find the needle than the paper but in a few minutes Dickie had written the following:

This dokkerment signed by us twins Richard and Mary Morton of 7 Brownlow Square, London, promises most solemn and faithful for all time that on this day in April (we haven't got the date) Harriet Sparrow also of London is made a member of the Lone Pine Club, and all the other older members of the Club promise and swear that this is true. Signed in our blood at Spaunton in Yorkshire in Grandpa Sparrow's new shop.

He sat back and read it through. Then with his penknife he sharpened a match-stick to a fine point. Mary passed him the needle, and after licking it he pricked the top of the third finger of his left hand and squeezed out a fat drop of blood. Then he dipped the match-stick several times in the blood of the Mortons and with some difficulty wrote RICHARD M.

Mary, with tightly closed eyes, next pricked her finger and wrote MARY M. and passed the document to Harriet.

"You're in now, Harry," she said as she sucked her finger. "When we get to Shropshire you'll have to sign in your own blood though."

The story you have just finished is one of the adventures of the members of the Lone Pine Club. Each adventure is complete in itself and there are now twenty of them. The complete list is as follows:

1. MYSTERY AT WITCHEND
2. SEVEN WHITE GATES
3. THE GAY DOLPHIN ADVENTURE
4. THE SECRET OF GREY WALLS
5. LONE PINE FIVE
6. THE ELUSIVE GRASSHOPPER
7. THE NEGLECTED MOUNTAIN
8. SAUCERS OVER THE MOOR
9. WINGS OVER WITCHEND
10. LONE PINE LONDON
11. THE SECRET OF THE GORGE
12. MYSTERY MINE
13. SEA WITCH COMES HOME
14. NOT SCARLET BUT GOLD
15. TREASURE AT AMORYS
16. MAN WITH THREE FINGERS
17. RYE ROYAL
18. STRANGERS AT WITCHEND
19. WHERE'S MY GIRL?
20. HOME TO WITCHEND

The author hopes that you have enjoyed this story and would like to know what you think of it. You can write to him, and he will answer your letter, which should be addressed to:

Malcolm Saville,
c/o Armada Books,
14 St. James's Place,
London SW1A 1PS.